Pedram Khosronejad (Ed.)

Women's Rituals and Ceremonies in Shiite Iran and Muslim Communities

Iranian Studies

edited by

Dr. Pedram Khosronejad
(University of St. Andrews)

Volume 1

LIT

Women's Rituals and Ceremonies in Shiite Iran and Muslim Communities

Methodological and theoretical challenges

edited by

Pedram Khosronejad

LIT

Cover image: Shrine near Lahijan, Gilan, Iran
©Khosronejad 1996

This book is printed on acid-free paper.

Bibliographic information published by the Deutsche Nationalbibliothek
The Deutsche Nationalbibliothek lists this publication in the Deutsche Nationalbibliografie; detailed bibliographic data are available in the Internet at http://dnb.d-nb.de.

ISBN 978-3-643-90605-2

A catalogue record for this book is available from the British Library

Klosbachstr. 107
CH-8032 Zürich
Tel. +41 (0) 44-251 75 05
Fax +41 (0) 44-251 75 06
E-Mail: zuerich@lit-verlag.ch
http://www.lit-verlag.ch

LIT VERLAG Dr. W. Hopf
Berlin 2015
Fresnostr. 2
D-48159 Münster
Tel. +49 (0) 2 51-62 03 20
Fax +49 (0) 2 51-23 19 72
E-Mail: lit@lit-verlag.de
http://www.lit-verlag.de

Distribution:
In the UK: Global Book Marketing, e-mail: mo@centralbooks.com
In North America: International Specialized Book Services, e-mail: orders@isbs.com
In Germany: LIT Verlag Fresnostr. 2, D-48159 Münster
Tel. +49 (0) 2 51-620 32 22, Fax +49 (0) 2 51-922 60 99,
E-mail: vertrieb@lit-verlag.de

In Austria: Medienlogistik Pichler-ÖBZ, e-mail: mlo@medien-logistik.at
e-books are available at www.litwebshop.de

یارب اندر وطن خویش غریب و زارم
من که در دیده یاران و عزیزان ،خوارم
نه انیسی که به او راز دل خویش کنم
نه طبیبی که کند چاره تن بیمارم
مادرم کو که زمانی ز ره مهر و وفا
شود از این همه اندوه گران غمخوارم

Oh Lord, I feel wretched and a stranger in my own land,
I, who in the eyes of my friends and dear ones appear so low and insignificant.
No bosom friend with whom I can unravel the secrets of my heart,
No physician who can tend to and cure my sick corps.
Where is my mother so that for a while and out of love and devotion,
Can share and alleviate all this heavy sorrows of mine.

Contents

Introduction

A major part of the Middle Eastern and North African experience have been said to be based on Muslim culture. But what is Muslim culture? As many Muslims say, Islam exists for all times and all places.[1] The Middle East and North African countries and societies cannot be defined as simply Muslim society, as more Muslims live in Indonesia, Bangladesh and India. Yet it is also clear that the territories of the Middle East or North Africa and the religion of Islam are closely intertwined: it was from Arabia that Islam originated and spread as the Prophet Muhammad's charismatic annunciation of a new shared belief system created a new mode of being in the world that permanently reconfigured the region's previously existing cultural models for living.[2]

Muslim societies encompass widely diverse religious and social structures and relations. Muslims seem to juggle local and multiple identities effortlessly – villager, tribesman, woman, citizen – with the broader identity of believer and to legitimize them all by reference to the idiom of the cosmopolitan community of believers (*umma*).[3] In spite of their diversity, their tenets share the basic core of beliefs and practices which Islam sets forth in the 'five pillars'. They enjoin the believers to bear witness to the oneness of God, to perform the five daily prayers, to fast during the month of Ramadan, to pay annual alms, and, if possible, to make the pilgrimage to Mecca at least once. Then one can conclude that Islam is more than a type of knowledge learned through reading Holy Quran, or listening to clerics or religious leaders. Orthodox statements of belief and formal rituals form only one part of the complicated structure of Islam.

Religious meaning must be constructed and reconstructed over and over. We can no longer accept that the 'appearance' of religion is inconsequential to the 'experience' of religion. The sensual elements of Islam

1 Lee Bowen and Early 2002, p. 3.
2 Lindholm 1996, p. 7.
3 Eickelman and Piscatori 1990, p. xiv.

are not merely decorations that mask belief; it is through the visible world that the invisible world becomes known and felt.[4]

Islam, the religion, exists as a definable, cross-culturally applicable entity: a set of religious beliefs which have been adopted and interpreted across the world depending on cultural context. The diversity of religious beliefs and practices in various Muslim societies has been a problem not only for the students of Islam, but for the Muslim community itself. In spite of the fact that Islam does not recognize any institutional religious authority or organization entrusted with defining the 'official' religious view, the relationship between 'official' and 'popular' religion has not disappeared, rather it has become more subtle and complex.

As Holy brings, the vitality and dynamism of Islam lies, in part, in receptivity to local custom and its ability to incorporate diverse customary practices. This ability of Islam to adapt itself to local traditions can be traced back to its very origin. Although Islam brought about a radical change in different societies, it did not outlaw all the pre-Islamic customs; rather, on the contrary, it incorporated many of them into its own system of law. This adaptability to local custom became even more significant when Islam gradually spread into areas with cultures radically different to those from which it originated.[5]

The awareness of alternatives to local belief and popular religion has, of course, increased more in recent years. Nowadays, hardly any Muslim community is effectively cut off from the wider society of which it is a part. Not only it is linked with the wider society or state through economic and political ties, it is also linked to its beliefs and ritual practices. In other words, we can see Islam as a uniform superstructure composed of the fundamentals of belief, with a diverse substructure of practices, cultures and their material manifestations below.

It was with this background and of course the main aim and objectives of the Centro Incontri Umani -to Encourage Understanding, Respect and Peace Internationally- that I decided to organize an international workshop on *Women, Rituals and Ceremonies in the Contemporary Muslim Communities and Islamic World* in Monte Verità (Ascona, Switzerland) between 8-10 June 2007.[6] With the full academic supports of Dr. A. Hobart, the di-

4 McDannell 1995, p. 272.

5 Holy 1991, p. 10.

6 At that time I was a Junior Research Fellow at the Middle East Centre of St. Antony's

rector of the Centro Incontri Umani, we invited nine female anthropologists whose specialty is in connection with the women rituals among Muslim societies. It was in this occasion that we also celebrated and honored Prof. Mary Elaine Hegland who dedicated most of her life and time to this field of anthropology.

At the workshop, during three days, the participants have presented and discussed different aspects of their field researches and experiences in regard to the women's rituals and devotional practices. One of our main aims in this program was to broaden our understanding of women's devotional life, as well as calling attention to its relation to general social change. Most of the presentations were based on field researches, direct observations and rituals participations. This gave us a unique opportunity to discuss methodological challenges related to gender issues and field research, to which we have dedicated one separate discussion session.

In our program, it was also important to address the relation between gender and ethnographical field researches in an Islamic research context. In the Islamic world and societies, social researchers, anthropologists and ethnographers do encounter many problems regarding their field works and activities. This matter increases when they want to work on female rituals, ceremonies, and social group activities. This important and main challenge is created by the fact that, contrary to male religious manifestations, commonly performed outdoors and sometimes indoors, female religious manifestations are mostly performed indoors. It is a space into which one has to negotiate access, and the gender of both the social actors and the researcher becomes a topic. Therefore, in our workshop the speakers have been encouraged to describe their perception of how their female gender has influenced their field work in a number of participant observational studies conducted by themselves in the last few years.

The following anthropologists made contributions to our workshop: Miriam Ali De Unzaga *(Female Weaving Rituals in Morocco: How Women Weavers Become Persons of Value)*, Ingvild Flaskerud *(Negotiating Ritual Participation and Performance – A Multicultural Experience)*, Pedram Khosronejad *(The Missing: Spiritual and Personal Loss in Bakhtiari Female Lamentation)*, Mary Elaine Hegland *(Women's Moharram Practices:*

College in the University of Oxford and a residential post-doctoral fellow at the Centro Incontri Umnai.

Expanding Opportunities in an Iranian Village), Sabine Kalinock *('Arus-i Qoraysh Ritual of Iranian Women: Fieldwork on Women's Ritual in Iran)*, Sawsan Karimi *(Home-ethnography of Women's Death Rituals in Bahrain)*, Su Min (*Remaking Pure Muslim Women: The Choice of lamentation and the Representation of Filial Piety After the Religious Reform of Islam*), Anna Neubauer *(Methodological implications of the Researcher's Gender and Religion: Reflexions on Fieldwork with Sufi Women in Istanbul)*, Faegheh Shirazi *(The Sofrih: Comfort and Community Among Women in Iran)*, Patricia Kelly Spurles (*Henna practices, gender and Islam in the life course in Marrakesh)*. That some of these studies are not included here in our collection is generally the author's own choice, the editor's decision, or because they were scheduled to appear elsewhere.

The main objective of this book is to study ritual performances to better understand how gender is constructed and comprehended. This study examines gender through the lens of collective rituals or ceremonial life in contemporary Muslim societies. The contribution of studies is not simply to extend the range of contexts in which gender can be analysed, but "'rather to demonstrate the significance of using gender as an analytic category to elucidate wider social, cultural and political process through ritual activities".[7]

Then, this collection should be considered as one of the first collective ethnographical publications in which authors present different aspects of female rituals and ceremonies among Muslim societies in countries such as Iran, China, Norway and Turkey. The chapters of this edited volume will examine the annual, seasonal, daily and occasional women's congregations in urban, rural and nomadic societies in the above-mentioned countries. Moreover, by comparing different aspects of female rituals in both Sunnite and Shi'ite communities, reader can find how other religions, such as Buddhism and Christianity, or local traditions and beliefs, such as African beliefs or even Sufism, can influence such rituals.

I would like to thank all the participants for an exceptionally good humoured and productive workshop which showed how rich the possibilities for further progress are in the anthropological studies of women rituals and ceremonies among Muslim societies.

My special thanks should go to Dr. A. Hobart, the director of Centro In-

7 Torab p. 2.

contri Umani who was my main supporter of this programme, for financing and organizing the workshop. Without her full support, I could never have run this programme and I want to express my sincere gratitude to her.

Bibliography

Eickelman, D. and James Piscatori (eds.). 1990. *Muslim travelers: pilgrimage, migration, and the religious imagination*. London; New York: Routledge.

Holy, L. 1993. *Religion and custom in a Muslim society: the Berti of Sudan*. Cambridge: Cambridge University Press.

Lee Bowen, D. and Evelyn A. Early (eds.). 2002. *Everyday life in the Muslim Middle East*. Bloomington: Indiana University Press.

Lindholm, C. 1996. *The Islamic Middle East: an historical anthropology*. Oxford; Cambridge, Mass: Blackwell Publishers.

McDannell, C. 1995. *Material Christianity: religion and popular culture in America*. New Haven; London: Yale University Press.

Torab, A. 2002, 'The politization of women's religious circles in post-revolutionary Iran'. In *Women, Religion and Culture in Iran* (eds) Sahra Ansari and Vanessa Martin, 143–68. Surrey: Curzon.

Reenacting the past, negotiating the present: *'Arus-i Qoraysh* ritual of Iranian women

Sabine Kalinock

Introduction

It was a casual remark from an Iranian friend, Narges, who was not part of any religious network, that raised my interest in the female-only ritual that I will analyse in this essay.[1] Hearing of my interest in women's religious gatherings, Narges recounted that she once played the 'bride of the Qoraysh' on the occasion of the birthday of the Prophet Muhammad's daughter Fatima. A religious relative who used to organize the ritual annually was unable to find another woman ready to play this role and so asked Narges, who agreed. She did not remember the whole course of the ritual, only that it included much merriment. She was required to dress completely in red and to 'faint' at just the right moment – still amused at the memory, she recalled that she performed this detail so realistically that some participants were afraid that something had happened to her. It was another year before I was given the opportunity to take part in the costumed play *'Arus-i Qoraysh* (bride of the Qoraysh, the dominant tribe of Mecca at the time of the Prophet).

The first months of my fieldwork coincided with the months of Muharram and Safar of the Islamic lunar calendar. Rituals in remembrance of the martyrdom of the third Shiite Imam, Hoseyn, constitute the climax of the liturgical year for the Twelver Shia. Hoseyn, the Prophet's grandson, was killed in the seventh century in Karbala, present-day Iraq. Ritual mourning dominates the public sphere. Religious and official buildings as well as

---

[1] This article is based on fieldwork conducted in Tehran and Shiraz, primarily between 2000 and 2002.

private homes are decorated with black banners. Large street processions organized by religious associations, called *hey'at*, fill the streets. People – women as well as men – gather in religious buildings erected especially for this purpose (*husayniyyeh*), in shrines (*imamzadeh*), in mosques and in private homes in order to listen to sermons and recitations (*rowzeh*) on the tragic fate of the Imam and his relatives, crying and ritually beating themselves. Passion plays (*ta'ziyeh*) are performed in public places and in *husayniyyehs*. Many women organize religious gatherings in their homes for three, seven or ten consecutive days. Rituals take place during the whole day at different places, starting before sunrise and continuing late into the night. During previous visits to Iran, I occasionally had been invited to *rowzeh* rituals. For a foreign researcher it is relatively easy to gain access to these religious gatherings. These experiences reinforced my perception of Shiism as a religion of mourning, as it is often described in the literature (Ayoub 1978; Keddie 1978; Fischer 1980).

It was only after long-term fieldwork that I realized that the Shiite ritual cycle for women was far more diverse (Torab 2006; Kalinock 2003b). In addition to mourning rituals that commemorate the days of the death of the Prophet, his daughter Fatima, the Imams and some of their relatives, there are also festive and joyous gatherings marking their birthdays. These rituals are called *mowludi* (from the Arabic word '*mawlud*', meaning 'birthday'). They include *mowludi-khani* the singing of joyous poems praising the Prophet and his family and expressing joy at their births. While a cantor recites the poems, the guests clap their hands. Some rituals also include the playing of the *daff* (frame drum). Additionally, pious families sometimes organize *mowludi-khani* at wedding parties to avoid secular forms of entertainment. Especially on these occasion, or those marking the birthday of the Prophet's daughter Fatima, *mowludi-khani* can be combined with a performance of the *'Arus-i Qorayshritual*.

To give an impression of the course and atmosphere of the gatherings, I will begin with a description of one *'Arus-i Qoraysh* ritual, which took place in northern Tehran in 2002. I will refer to other genres of dramatic performance in Iran as well as to historical sources.

'*Arus-i Qoraysh* in the north of Tehran

The ritual took place in one of the wealthier parts of the north of Tehran. The hostess, Afsaneh, head of a bank, described herself as pious and told me that she tries to observe all religious duties. She had organized the ritual in fulfilment of a vow made after her husband had recovered from a surgery. All of the nearly fifty female guests – relatives, friends, colleagues and neighbours – were dressed well; many were wearing a short skirt and sleeveless top.

Figure 1 Women are carrying the trays for the wedding of Qasim, mourning ritual during Muharram, Shiraz© Kalinock 2002

The woman leading the ritual, addressed as *khanom* ('lady' – a polite form of address) by the hostess, arrived together with three female assistants at about four o'clock in the afternoon. She began with the recitation of invocations (*do'ayi faraj-i Imam-i zaman* and others), followed by the singing of *mowludi* poems. While the cantor chanted joyous poems praising Fatima, the assistants played the *daff*, and one woman thumped the rhythm on a brass tray. After invocations for the hostess and for her relatives and guests who had special wishes, the *khanom-i jalasih*[2] announced that she required the help of a *siyyidah* (a female descendant of the Prophet's family) as well as seven other women and girls. The *khanom-i jalasih* gave the eight women and girls some garments, and they went to an adjoining room to change clothes.

Three younger women dressed all in red. Each was wearing a short *fustanella*, harem pants, a vest and a headband; one of them was also wearing a transparent headscarf. They represented the bride of the Qoraysh and two of her servants. Two girls were dressed in the same way but all in white; two others were dressed completely in green. They represented the *huris* and angels. The *seyyidih* was asked to perform the ritual ablution first. When she returned, she was wearing a long green dress, a crown with imitation diamonds and a transparent face veil.

First, the bride of the Qoraysh entered the room with her two servants. She sat on a chair in front of the *khanom-i jalasih,* facing the guests. On a tray in front of her the hostess had arranged paraphernalia for the *hammam*. The preparation of the bride for the wedding night was translated in pantomime. One of the assistants of the *khanom-i jalasih* began to rub the bride's body symbolically with flannel, removing her facial and body hair. The guests clapped their hands and exclaimed. While she pantomimed plucking the facial hair, the assistant sang:

hala bandash mindazih	Now she plucks the facial hair

The guests repeated the chorus four times:

bindaz, bindaz	Pluck it, pluck it!

Then the assistant took an oversized pair of scissors, singing:

hala abru michineh	Now she plucks the eyebrows

And the guests repeated the chorus again:

2 The term commonly used for the woman leading the ritual is "*khanom-i jalasih*" (lady of the gathering).

bechin, bechin	Pluck it, pluck it!

The assistants and the bride bent forward and back rhythmically. Then the women pantomimed the painting of the bride's face, accompanied by the same way of singing:

hala wasmih mikishih	Now she applies *wasmih*[3]
bikish, bikish, bikish, bikish	apply it, apply it, apply it, apply it
hala sormih mikishi	Now she applies kohl
bikish, bikish, bikish, bikish	apply it, apply it, apply it, apply it!

The other traditional items mentioned for the face painting were *sifidab* (white powder) and *sorkhab* (powdered red marble to redden the face), complemented by *matik* (lipstick) and *rimel* (mascara). The assistant painted rouge and lipstick on the bride's face excessively. The grotesque appearance and dancing of the bride were accompanied by loud hand clapping.

The singing and dancing then stopped, the light was turned off and candles were lit. The *khanom-i jalasih* started to tell the story of the *'Arus-i Qoraysh*:

One of girls of the Qoraysh was going to be married. Her family invited Hazrat-i Zahra to their wedding party. They wanted to boast in front of Hazrat-i Zahra about their wealth and the splendour of the wedding celebration and humiliate her. They knew that Hazrat-i Zahra did not dispose of any festive dress. Hazrat-i Zahra perceived their bad intent and refused the invitation. The angel Gabriel came down on earth to the Prophet, instructing him to prompt Hazrat-i Zahra to go to the wedding party. He told the Prophet: 'God will provide her with splendour and glory so that the members of the Qoraysh will be astounded.' The angels and *huris* appeared from heaven and adorned Hazrat-i Zahra in the most splendorous garments.

At that moment, the *seyyidih*, representing Hazrat-i Zahra entered the

3 Traditionally, a preparation made from indigo leaves was used to dye the bride's eyebrows dark blue. See Mottahedin and Yaghmayi 1993.

room, followed by the girls dressed in green and white. The girls were holding each other's hands. Each girl was also holding a rose. The *khanom-i jalasih* continued with the story:

When the family of the Qoraysh saw the dignity and brilliance of Hazrat-i Zahra they felt humble and wretched. Their plan was destroyed. They prostrated before Hazrat-i Zahra. When the bride of the Qoraysh saw the glory of Hazrat-i Zahra, she fainted. All supposed that she had died. Hazrat-i Zahra went near her, and she awoke to new life. She also prostrated before Hazrat-i Zahra, paid homage to her and converted to Islam. All the other women converted, too.

This scene was also enacted. The bride uttered a sigh of astonishment and sank down. Fatima woke her and then sat on the chair where the bride of the Qoraysh had been sitting. The women and girls lined up behind her, the bride standing at the very back.

The *khanom-i jalasih* now asked the *seyyidih* to say two verses (*rak'at*) of the prayers. Some of the guests went to the *seyyidih* to ask her to pray for them (*eltemas-i do'a*). Some touched her head and hands, uttering invocations for the fulfilment of their wishes. Then the light was turned on, the two assistants of the *khanom-i jalasih* played the *daff* and the girls danced around the *seyyidih,* who represented Fatima. The hostess and the *khanom-i jalasih* were throwing candies, which the guests put in their handbags.

At the end, the women and girls returned the clothes to the *khanom-i jalasih.* She asked the girls to keep the roses until their wishes were fulfilled. Then she handed a bunch of flowers to the *seyyidih.* Again, the *khanom-i jalasih* took the microphone; she now sang modern Persian pop songs. The guests clapped their hands, and some danced. About half an hour later, the *khanom-i jalasih* ended her performance and put on her scarf and *Chador*. The hostess gave her an envelope containing about 100 € (80.000 Toman), and she left.

The course of the ritual

Compared to *mowludi* rituals in general, the bride of the Qoraysh ritual is performed less frequently. During my fieldwork, I was able to take part in two additional rituals. One differed mainly in details; the other one was performed incompletely. All three rituals took place at the homes of women from the middle or upper class. The main reason for this is certainly connected with the high costs: the hostess must pay not only the woman leading the ritual but also her assistants. Furthermore, props, such as clothing for the performers of Hazrat-i Zahra, the bride and the angels and *huris*, are needed. I was told that only a limited number of groups perform this ritual, which allows them to demand high fees.

Although there is a kind of professionalization at work, these groups do not play the roles themselves. For pious women, it is not a theatrical play that demands the actors to play their roles as competently as possible, but a religious ritual. Women who represent one of the holy beings are able to gain religious merit.

In Iran, different genres of dramatic performances exist. The most well-known are the Persian passion plays *ta'ziyeh*. In Persian literature, *'Arus-i Qoraysh* is most often mentioned in connection with *ta'ziyeh*. In *ta'ziyeh*, as well as in *'Arus-i Qoraysh*, costumed performers re-enact conflicts between members of the Prophet's family and their enemies. The most striking outward similarity between the two is the colour symbolism. The negative characters are dressed all in red; the positive ones in green or white. Persian literature mentions *ta'ziyeh* performed by women of nobility during the time of the Qajars (1785–1925), yet only one of my consultants had taken part in *ta'ziyeh* of and for women in northern Iran (Khatirat-i Munis al-Dowlih 2001, 96; Beyzayi 1966, 160ff.). During one female mourning ritual in the month of Muharram, women re-enacted the wedding of Qasim, the son of Imam Hassan, who was killed in Karbala on the day of his wedding (Flaskerud 2005). In public *ta'ziyehs,* even female roles are performed by men. Whereas *ta'ziyeh* deals primarily with the tragic events in Karbala and the martyrdom of Imam Hoseyn and his relatives, and takes place primarily during the month of Muharram, *'Arus-i Qoraysh* has a 'happy ending' and is performed on feast days.[4]

'Arus-i Qoraysh, like *ta'ziyeh,* refers to a historic conflict. While some of the clans of the Qoraysh were wealthy, the clan of the Prophet, the Bani Hashem, suffered from poverty. One *khanom-i jalasih* explained to me after the ritual that it was the wife of Abu Lahab and her female relatives who had invited Fatima to their wedding party. Abu Lahab was a fierce enemy of

---

4 Beyzayi 1966, 161f., mentions that during the times of the Qajars there were also comical *ta'ziyeh* (*ta'ziyeh mazhak*) that made fun of the enemies of the Prophet's family.

the Prophet. He and his wife are the only persons who are cursed by name, in Surat 111 of the Quran.

Between secular and sacred – hilarious and solemn – challenge and commitment

The performance of *'Arus-i Qoraysh* is split into two parts. In the first part the singing, together with the costumed play, describes the traditional preparation of the bride for the wedding night – which can also be found in Persian sources (Katirayi 1999, 165–68; Mottahedin and Yagmai 1993). In traditional families it was, and still is, not customary for an unmarried girl to use makeup. Shortly before the wedding she undergoes a beauty treatment: her body hair is removed, she is made up and given a new hairstyle. This represents a purification and separation rite, marking the change of status from unmarried girl to married woman. It emphasizes that the beauty of a woman is reserved for her husband.

The first part of the ritual thus addresses a situation with which the women are familiar; through exaggeration, it is ridiculed. The performance can be seen as a critique of gender roles that emphasize that the beauty of a woman serves to please her husband. This especially applies when the ritual is performed in the context of a wedding party, in the presence of women who underwent the same treatment. In this part of the ritual, the women do not distinguish themselves from the faithless bride; rather, they become wedding guests and can identify with her. It is a moment of communitas in the sense of Victor Turner.

The preparation of the bride was the most elaborate part of the ritual and was characterized by a hilarious mood. The women joined in the chorus, crowed and whistled, clapped their hands and laughed about the funny appearance of the bride. The atmosphere reminded me of the different forms of traditional Persian improvisation theatre, like the *baziha-yi nemayishi* (theatrical plays of women) or *ruhowzi* (improvisation theatre of exclusively male performers) that have also been performed at weddings. Both have comical content, often containing sexual allusions and questioning social norms.[5] For example, in one of the *baziha-yi nemayishi*, which recently

[5] *Ruhowzi* was performed especially at weddings and circumcision celebrations. The main character is a clown that makes fun of dignitaries; all female roles were played by

have become fashionable among younger women, a woman in labour puzzles over the probable father of her child. The American anthropologist Beeman writes about *ruhowzi* performed by men:

It mocks and attacks the whole fabric of social and sexual structures which bind the spectators in their everyday life, and rather than washing the pressures of life away in sea of tears, it aims to dispel those pressures in gales of laughter – the louder and longer the better (Beeman 1981, 379).

The shift to the second part of the ritual is cued visually by turning off the lights and lighting candles. Whereas the recitative in the first part was led by one of the assistants, the narration was recounted by the *khanom-i jalasih*. The hilarious mood changed to a more solemn one. The participants now became the followers of Fatima, who accompany her to her enemies. The different roles of the participants in *ta'ziyeh* are also highlighted by Beeman:

Those in the audience in *ta'ziyeh* are placed in the position of being both the symbolic murderers of Hoseyn in Karbala and being the mourners of Hoseyn after his death. At the conclusion of the performance they must end up being converted, or renewed, through their profound expression of grief at Hoseyn's death, and through their demonstrations of loyalty to the ideological order that Hoseyn represents (Beeman 1979, 30).

The ritual participants are, during the first part of the wedding, guests of the bride of the Qoraysh, then of the retinue of Fatima. Like *ta'ziyeh*, the ritual allows the participants 'to renew their commitment to a religious and ideological order of which they are already an integral part' (Beeman 1979, 30; cf. Ayoub 1978, 149.).

Ta'ziyeh emphasizes mourning and empathy with the tragic fate of Hoseyn and his family and followers, who died as martyrs or became captives. Gratification and recreation of justice is transferred to the future and the hereafter. '*Arus-i Qoraysh* also deals with wealth and poverty, power and weakness, humiliation and retaliation – but it is Fatima who prevails.[6]

men. Since the Islamic revolution, public performances have been forbidden. For further explanation, see Beeman 1981; Beyzayi 1966, 166ff. The *baziha-yi nemayishi* also has been performed at weddings and circumcision celebrations, by women for other women. They often spoof and question gender roles. The term '*baziha-yi nemayishi*' has been coined by the Iranian folklorist Anjavi-Shirazi. See Anjavi-Shirazi 1973; Safa-Isfahani 1980; Shay 1995.

6 For *ta'ziyeh* see Ayoub 1978, 48.

By virtue of her rank as the Prophet's daughter, her purity and her faith, she overwhelms the politically and economically powerful. This also gives the participants the feeling that their belief is true and superior. The ritual expresses the hope that a pious and virtuous life is rewarded in this life. This hope and perception also plays a central role in other female rituals, which are nearly always performed in connection with a vow (*nazr*) (e.g., Betteridge 1980; Kalinock 2003a.).

Through the performance, an incident from the past is brought to the present. The women are onlookers as well as participants in the wedding of the bride of the Qoraysh; they are in the present as well as in the past. They are in a liminal state in the sense of Victor Turner. Several women explained to me that it is impossible to act as Fatima. The woman who represents her, therefore, wears a face veil. Several publications about *ta'ziyeh* point out that the performers deliberately distance themselves from their role. Mamnoun emphasizes that, for a pious Shiite Muslim, identification with the Prophet, his daughter Fatima and the Imams, who are infallible – or with their enemies, who are monstrously bad – is impossible; they only represent them.[7]

At the same time, the participants believe that the woman who represents Fatima possesses a special power for the duration of the ritual. The women were convinced that the wishes made by the women representing Fatima, the angels and the *huris* would surely be fulfilled. In the ritual described here, several participants touched Fatima's head and hands like they would touch the bars of a sanctuary. In the other ritual, women who wanted to utter a wish sat in the chair where Fatima had been sitting. An equation between the character of the performer and the role appears. Several women told me that Fatima, as well as the *huris* and the angels, should be represented by women who are *seyyidihs*, descendants of the Prophet's family. It is more difficult to find someone who is prepared to play the role of the bride of the Qoraysh, just as it is more difficult to find someone to play the role of Hoseyn's enemies in *ta'ziyeh.*

The presentation of Fatima in the narration corresponds with her rep-

---

7 Mamnoun 1967, 159. Yet, Chelkowski 2002 also states: 'Influenced heavily by the realistic acting of modern film and television, *ta'ziyeh* actors no longer distance themselves from the characters that they are playing, but throw themselves wholeheartedly into their roles. Often the performers identify so strongly with their parts that they are swept away by their situations.'

resentation as a role model. She follows a humble lifestyle without any luxury and is an obedient daughter. The critique of the exaggerated display of wealth and lavishness at weddings is also part of everyday discourse. Women often complained that social pressure and fear of gossip forces them to spend a significant amount of money on the wedding celebration. At another ritual, the *khanom-i jalasih* answered, 'Hazrat-i Zahra had no crystal glass and no carpets from Isfahan. On the day of her wedding she gave all her clothes and jewellery to the poor.' As in the narration, a religious ideal is contrasted with social reality:

> *Ta'ziyeh* by holding up the ideal moral order for all to see, reminds everybody of the terrible degree to which society falls short of its high and uncompromising standards; it thus compels man to change, urging him to move closer to the core of the moral order (Beeman 1979, 381).

Yet in the narration, the religiousness of Fatima alone is not sufficient to crow over the women of the Qoraysh. Earthly luxury is also required: *huris* and angels attire Fatima in festive dress and adorn her like a queen with a crown. The women of the Qoraysh are hoisted by their own petard. This secular Cinderella motif – a poor but kind-hearted woman receives the help of supernatural forces in a conflict with more powerful persons – is also part of other female rituals in Iran, like the *sofrih-yi Bibi Sih Shanbih*, a ritual meal dedicated to supernatural beings of unclear origin (Torab 2005; Kalinock 2003a; Jamzadeh and Mills 1986).

The second part of the *'Arus-i Qoraysh* ritual does not question the gender roles in general. However, Fatima takes a more active role than in *ta'ziyeh,* in which she is, for example, depicted as a mother crying for her sons, Hassan and Hoseyn, whose martyrdom she foretells. The conflict arises between women and is solved by a woman: it is through Fatima that all women convert to Islam. Fatima plays a central role in Shiite religion in general. She is the mother of all Imams, and she belongs to the *chahardah ma'sum*, the fourteen Infallible Ones (as does the Prophet). In times of crisis, women often invoke her for help. Many vows are dedicated to Fatima. The women frequently explained that, as a woman herself, she better understands women's hardships.

Beeman describes the Persian Passion play *ta'ziyeh* and the comical improvisation theatre *ruhowzi* as two complementary poles. *Ta'ziyeh* is sacral and confirms the ideal moral order, whereas *ruhowzi* is secular and questions social norms. *'Arus-i Qoraysh* can be seen as an alliance of the two. The first part of the ritual is accompanied by loud laughter, and the play expresses criticism of social norms. In the second part the atmosphere changed – some women started to cry when they saw the woman representing Fatima, or when they asked her to pray for them. Criticism refers to the others – the faithless Arab bride and her following – whereas the participants are called on to behave in accordance with the religious moral order.

'Arus-i Qoraysh in Persian literature: a comparison

From Persian sources one can conclude that the ritual was much more popular during the time of the Qajars, until the first half of the twentieth century. The Persian anthropologist Katirayi equates *mowludi* with *'Arus-i Qoraysh* and explains that the ritual was once performed by religious families at weddings and throughout the year, in fulfilment of a vow (Katirayi 1999; Mo'in 1992). Anaseri dates the ritual to the time of the Qajars (Anaseri 1987); this assumption is supported by the clothes that the women performers wore during the ritual: the short *fustanella* and the harem pants common at that time. *Ta'ziyeh* also reached its peak during the time of the Qajars. Beyzayi states that *'Arus-i Qoraysh* was very popular among the women of the court of Naser al-Din Shah (1848–1896). Their laughter, he quotes, was heard in the nearby bazaar. Directly following the *'Arus-i Qoraysh* ritual, the *ta'ziyeh* of the wedding of Qasim was performed. Qasim, the son of Imam Hassan, was killed in Karbala on his wedding night. Thus, laughter was followed by ritual crying.[8] As mentioned before, the wedding of Qasim is also the only scene that I saw performed at a women's *rowzeh*.

A detailed description of the ritual can be found in the memoirs of Munis al-Dowlih, who stayed in the harem of Naser al-Din Shah (1831–1896). Munis al-Dowlih describes *'Arus-i Qoraysh* as being very popular. The performance also attracted women from surrounding cities to Tehran. According to her description, the women of the Qoraysh wore ludicrous red clothing. Some wrapped saddlecloths around their bodies and were riding donkeys.[9] The play began with a scene that showed Fatima baking bread, thinking about the invitation to the wedding and deciding not to attend. A

8 Beyzayi 1966, 162–63. For the performance of the wedding of Qasim (the son of Imam Hasan) at women's rituals in Shiraz, see Flaskerud 2005.

9 *'Palun-i olaq push'* (person wearing a saddlecloth) is also a humiliating insult.

woman wearing angel wings represented the angel Gabriel. She sent for the *huris*, and twelve girls appeared, vesting Fatima in glorious attire and accompanying her to the wedding. The *daff* was played, *esfand* and incense were burned and rose water was sprayed. The further course of the ritual is in accordance with the course of the ritual described above.

The plot of the story is the same as is told today, but in the older version additional scenes are enacted: Fatima at home, the appearance of the angel Gabriel and the clothing of Fatima. Unlike today, in the description of Munis al-Dowlih the story of the bride of the Qoraysh is not narrated by a *khanom-i jalasih* and translated into pantomime by the women, but every woman speaks her own text in verse. This oral tradition seems to be lost. In the memoirs of Munis al-Dowlih, the preparation of the bride is not mentioned. Probably in former times it was not part of the ritual. As mentioned above, there was a clear distinction between the first and second parts of the ritual. The hilarious atmosphere, the grotesque dancing and the inherent critique of gender roles are reminiscent of the secular theatrical plays of women (*baziha-yi nemayishi*). In all three rituals in which I took part, the first part was the longest, with the greatest interaction of the participants. Interestingly, at the ritual that was performed only incompletely, this part was enacted with all of the details, whereas the second part was not performed at all – and Fatima did not appear in it. The hostess had told the guests at the beginning that her wish uttered at an *'Arus-i Qoraysh* ritual had been granted and that she had vowed to organize the same ritual. Obviously, she had tried to reconstruct the ritual from her memory. Neither the hostess nor the women who participated were familiar with the religious background. This became especially obvious when the guests sat on the chair where the 'unfaithful' bride had been sitting to make their vows. Form and intent (the fulfilment of vows) subsisted; the religious meaning was lost.

Concluding remarks

Shiite rituals in general are characterized by few rules and regulations; there are many possibilities for innovation and individual creativity. This is especially true for women's rituals that take place in the private atmosphere of the home, where only invited guests have access – like most *mowludi* and *'Arus-i Qoraysh* rituals. The reasons to organize, to lead, or to take part in a religious gathering are manifold. The women themselves often named their love for the *chahardah ma'sum* as the main reason for their involvement. The rituals allow them to earn religious merit (*savab*). The hostess can transfer economic resources into religious and social esteem. Participants use the rituals to initiate vows, to benefit from religious education, to socialise with other women and strengthen their social networks, or simply to have fun. Ritual crying can serve as a form of catharsis.

At the same time, religious rituals are places for political discourse. The way a ritual is held contains a political statement. Hilarious singing and playing of the daff are normally not found at rituals organized by women near to the Islamic government in Iran. Due to the restriction of leisure activities in the Islamic Republic, religious gatherings have also gained attractiveness among women who have not been part of the religious networks previously. Furthermore, since the Islamic revolution religious gatherings have offered women one of few possibilities to demonstrate their abilities and earn money. Well-known women preachers and cantors (*maddah*) dispose of great social and religious esteem, wide social networks, influence, mobility and financial means. One of the cantors I regularly accompanied was a singer on a television show at the time of the last Shah of Iran. In an interview with a Persian journalist, a woman described her decision to become a *maddah*:

> "I saw what is required by our society. Imagine that I had become a singer. My husband would have said: 'Where have you been till now?' But now that I follow the way of religion, the way of Islam, there are no restrictions. Sometimes I only return late in night. Even if I had a concert in *Talar-i Vahdat* [the main concert hall in Tehran] would I be allowed to stay away from home till late in the night? Definitely not. If you want to become a singer there are endless difficulties, you need permission and all these things. For a *maddah* it is easy, she needs no certificate and knows no restrictions."[10]

This might also explain why in the example above the cantor herself sang pop songs.

I want to end with another instance concerning *'Arus-i Qoraysh*: a secular Iranian friend, Nastaran, who grew up in a leftist intellectual family, recounted that she once accompanied her pious sister-in-law to a *mowludi* in the context of a wedding party. As a sign of honour to her sister-in-law,

---

[10] Interview of the Iranian journalist Qotbi Yaqubi with a *maddah* in 2002, unpublished manuscript.

Nastaran was chosen as Fatima. Nastaran was bewildered when, after the rituals, several women came to her kiss her hands and ask her to pray for them. She had actively participated in the ritual but remained emotionally unaffected. Wirth writes about *ta'ziyeh*: 'Ta'ziyeh focuses not on producing signs but on producing signs for believers' (Wirth 1979, 36.). This is also true for *'Arus-i Qoraysh* – these signs are no more understood by all participants. This example demonstrates the different and manifold attitudes and perceptions of the participants. Some women believe in the religious potency of the ritual, others are more or less spectators who follow the course with amusement, like the ritual is a theatre play. *Ta'ziyeh* has undergone a similar development. In the 1960s and '70s, intellectuals and artists discovered *ta'ziyeh* as an art form. Presently, performances of *ta'ziyeh* and *'Arus-i Qoraysh* are also part of theatre festivals in Tehran. The deep emotional and religious experience is no longer shared by all participants.

The different perspectives and personal experiences of participants at a funeral ritual in Trinidad is analysed by Gerholm.[11] One participant knows the theoretical 'meaning' of the ritual but remains an outsider. His relatives know little about their own ritual but are touched emotionally. Gerholm states: 'They all live in a fragmented cultural universe combining elements of various cultural systems' (Gerholm 1988, 194). This is also true for Iran.

Bibliography

Anaseri, J. 1987. *Namayish va niyayish dar Iran*. Tehran: Nima.

Anjavi-Shirazi, S. 1973. *Baziha-yi namayishi*. Tehran: Amir Kabir.

Ayoub, M. 1978. *Redemptive Suffering in Islam: A Study of the Devotional Aspects of ᶜ'Ashura' in Twelver Shiᶜism*. The Hague, Paris, New York: Mouton Publishers.

Beeman, W. O 1979 'Cultural dimensions of performance conventions in Iranian ta'ziyeh'. In *Ta'ziyeh: Ritual and Drama in Iran* (ed.) P. J. Chelkowski, 24–31. New York: New York University Press.

——— 1981 'A full arena: the development and meaning of popular performance traditions in Iran'. In *Modern Iran: The Dialectics of Continuity and Change* (eds) M. Bonine and N. R. Keddie, 285–305. Albany: New York State University Press.

Bell, C. 1992. *Ritual Theory, Ritual Practice*. New York: Oxford University Press.

[11] Gerholm 1988. He refers to a ritual that the writer Naipaul describes.

Betteridge, A. H. 1980. 'The controversial vows of urban women in Iran'. In *Unspoken Worlds: Women's Religious Lives in Non-Western Cultures* (eds.) N. Auer Falks and R.M. Gross, 141–58. San Francisco: Harper and Row.

Beyzayi, B. 1966. *Namayish dar Iran*. Tehran: Kavian.

Chelkowski, P. J. 1979. *Ta'ziyeh: Ritual Drama in Iran*. New York: New York University Press.

———, P. J. 2002. 'Time out of memory: *ta'ziyeh*, the total drama'. asiasociety.org/arts/taziyeh/chelkowski.html.

Fischer, M. M. J. 1980. *Iran : From Religious Dispute to Revolution*. Cambridge: Harvard University Press.

Flaskerud, I. 2005. 'Oh, my heart is sad. It is Moharram, the month of Zaynab: aesthetics and women's mourning ceremonies in Shiraz'. In *The Gender Dynamics of Ritual Performances and Symbolic Discourses of Modern Shi'i Islam* (ed.) K. S. Aghaie, 65–91. Austen: The University of Texas Press.

Gerholm, T. 1988. 'On ritual: a postmodern view'. *Ethnos* 3: 190–203.

Hegland, M. 1983, 'Two images of Hussain: accommodation and revolution in an Iranian Village'. In *Religion and Politics in Iran: Shi 'ism from Quietism to Revolution* (ed.) N. R. Keddie, 218–35. New Haven: Yale University Press.

Jamzadeh, L., and M. Mills. 1986. 'Iranian sofrih: from collective to female ritual'. In *Gender and Religion: On the Complexity of Symbols* (eds.) C. W. Bynum, S. Harrell and P. Richman, 23–65. Boston: Beacon Press.

Kalinock, S. 2003a. 'Supernatural intercession to earthly problems: *sofrih* rituals among Shiite Muslims and Zoroastrians in Iran'. In *Zoroastrian Rituals in Context (Studies in the History of Religions)*, 531–47. Leiden: Brill.

———. 2003b. 'Between party and devotion: 'Mowludi of women in Tehran'. *Critique: Critical Studies of the Middle East* 12, no. 2: 173–87.

———. 2004. 'Touching a sensitive topic: research on Shiite rituals of women'. *Iranian Studies, The Journal of the Society for Iranian Studies* 37, no. 4: 665–674.

Kamalkhani, Z. 1996. *Women's Islam: Religious Practice among Women in Today's Iran*. Ph.D. dissertation, University of Bergen.

Keddie. N. 1978. *Scholars Saints and Sufis: Muslim Religious Institutions Since 1500*. California: University of California Press.

Katirayi, M. 1999. *Az khisht ta khisht*. Tehran: Nashr-i Salis.

Mamnoun, P. 1967. *Tazija. Schiitisch-persisches Passionspiel*. Vienna: Notring.

Mo'in, M. 1992. 'Mowludi'. In *Farhang-i Farsi*, 4449. Tehran: Nashr-i Talish.

Mottahedeh, N. 2005. 'Karbala drag kings and queens'. *Drama Review* 49, no. 4: 73–85.

Mottahedin, S., and E. Yaghmayi, 1993, 'Cosmetics'. *Encyclopaedia Iranica Online*.

Sa'd-u Nadiyan, S. (ed.). 2001. *Khatirat-i Munis al-Dowlih* . Tehran: Zarrin.

Safa-Isfahani, K. 1980. 'Female centered world views in Iranian culture: symbolic representations of sexuality in dramatic games'. *Signs: Journal of Women in Culture and Society* 6, no. 11: 33–53.

Shay, A. 1995. 'Baziha-yi Namayishi: Iranian women's theatrical plays'. *Dance Research Journal* 27, no. 2: page range.

Thaiss, G. 1972. 'Religious symbolism and social change: the drama of Hoseyn'. In *Scholars, Saints and Sufis: Muslim Religious Institutions in the Middle East since 1500* (ed.) N. R. Keddie, 349–66. Berkeley: University of California Press.

Torab, A. 1996. 'Piety as gendered agency: a study of Jalaseh ritual discourse in Iran'. *Journal of the Royal Anthropological Institute* 2: 235–52.

———. 2005. 'Vows, mediumship and gender: women's votive meals in Iran'. In Gender, Religion and Change in the Middle East (eds.) I. M. Okkenhaug and I. Flaskerud, 207–22. Oxford: Berg Publishers.

———. 2006. *Performing Islam: Gender and Ritual in Iran*. Boston: Brill Academic Publishers.

Turner, V. 1969. *The Ritual Process: Structure and Anti-structure*. Chicago: Aldine.

Wirth, A. 1979. 'Semiological aspects of the ta'ziyyeh'. In *Ta'ziyeh: Ritual and Drama in Iran* (ed.) P. J. Chelkowski, 32–44. New York: New York University Press.

Sofrih and *walima*: food as ritual in the Islamic Republic of Iran

Faegheh Shirazi

Throughout human history, food has enjoyed a direct association with magic, medicinal potency and healing. In addition to its basic role of supporting physical health, food has been used across cultures to mark identity, celebrate ritual and invoke divine blessing or favour. This chapter focuses primarily on the differences and similarities between two food-centred events in Iran: *sofrih* and *walima*. While *sofrih* is usually private and gender-exclusive, *walima* is open to all, is announced to the general public and has acquired a strongly religious connotation over the past several decades.

In Iranian (Persian)[1] culture, *sofrih* (pronounced 'soff-reh', with emphasis on the aspirated 'h') is a generic term for any cloth on which food is served. In traditional Iranian culture, families gather around the *sofrih* for meals that are spread on the floor. This everyday meal is known as *Sofrih-i ghaza*. The term '*sofrih*' carries additional meanings, including:

"... a party in which a meal is served to invited guests, and *Sofrih-i dil* (spread of the heart) means confiding one's innermost thoughts and feelings. *Sofrih-i nazri* refers to the *sofrih* used for a ceremonial votive meal (*ghazay-i nazri*) given to honor a saint or pray for a certain outcome."[2]

Other types of popular *sofrihs* customary among Iranian people are *Sofrih-i aghd*, a special spread arranged exclusively for a marriage ceremony, and *Sofrih-i haftsin* (also known as *Sofrih-i Nowruz*), a spread arranged for the

---

1 I use 'Iranian' and 'Persian' interchangeably, as it is not possible to separate the greater culture of Persia from the land of Iran.

2 Shirazi 2005, 293.

occasion of the Iranian new year, *Nowruz*. *Sofrih-i nowruz* is kept for a duration of thirteen days, from the first to the thirteenth day of Farvardin (21March), which is the first month in the Iranian calendar (beginning of spring).

Some may describe the Iranian relationship with food, especially where the *sofrih* is concerned, as 'democratic'. That is, the same type of foods are eaten by rich and poor alike, in urban and rural environments, although, arguably, the quantity and portions of the food, as well as the utensils and serving dishes, may vary according to each household's resources. Nevertheless, perhaps this 'democratic' aspect reveals an egalitarian predisposition at the core of Persian society.

The Persian word '*sur*' refers to a festive, lavish meal celebrating a joyous occasion, such as the completion of a large project, acquiring a new job or welcoming the good news of a birth. At such times, when one wants to share the happy occasion with friends and family, one will give a *sur*. In this way, *sur* is always associated with a sumptuous meal enjoyed by invited guests.[3] Thus, the act of *Sur dadan,* or giving a party, is not especially related to any religious ideology or ritual.

Likewise, the Arabic word *walima* also refers to the abundant quality of a meal or banquet. In fact, *walima* literally translates as 'lavish meal'. Neither *sur* nor *walima* carry any specific religious requirement. However, since the establishment of the Islamic Republic of Iran in 1978, *walima* has acquired a religious overtone. The word '*walima*' now refers to a banquet honouring (and usually hosted by) those individuals who have successfully completed the Hajj pilgrimage to Mecca, one of the pillars of Islam.

Over the past thirty years or so, other Muslim groups (in India, Pakistan and Bangladesh, for example) have also ascribed a religious significance to *walima,* using the term to refer to the wedding banquet following an Islamic marriage ceremony (*nikah*). In fact, Dihkhoda's encyclopaedic Persian dictionary defines *walima* as:

"A marriage feast, a feast given for happy occasions, a feast given to a group of people (formally invited or just drop in uninvited) for a festive meal...according

3 The word '*sur*' in Avestan and Pahlavi means 'daily', 'breakfast', 'morning' or 'meal'. In many Iranian dialects, such as Baluchi, '*sir*' means 'wedding' or 'engagement'. In today's Iranian society, the dialect spoken by Zoroastrians uses '*sur*' to mean 'wedding'. Other terms, such as *sur chiran*, similar to 'food freeloader' in English, suggest the close relationship between *sur* and food.

to Ibin Hajar *walima* is used for the ceremony of *nikah* [Muslim marriage]... other common usage of the word is for example: *walima* for *khatnih* (a boy's circumcision), ... according to the Prophet *walima* is given in five occasions: for a marriage, after having a child, for a circumcision ceremony, in the occasion of buying a new house and after returning from Mecca [performance of hajj] (Dihkhoda 1994, 20554)."

After the Islamic Revolution of 1978, when Iran experienced drastic social change, a substantial number of Arabic words were adopted into popular use. Many of these words were introduced through clerics' sermons or via multiple forms of visual media.[4] Perhaps no cleric was more influential in promoting this process than Ayatollah Khomeyni, one of the most visible public figures of his time and an individual who continues to exert strong influence in Iran many years after his death.[5]

walima, a term now synonymous with a religious ritual feast, represents one of the Arabic words introduced into Persian popular culture. In contemporary Iran, the *walima* celebration has assumed an exceptionally high level of visibility, with banners announcing the event hung outside the banquet site. The site may be a private residence, catering locale, or restaurant. This display of banners usually contains congratulatory messages, acknowledging the names of the *haji* (male) and *hajiah* (female) who have returned from the most important pilgrimage of their lives.

In contrast, *sofrih* remains a very private event, eschewing any form of public announcement. Like the *sofrih*, a *walima* is attended by private invitation only. However, if a person walks into a *walima* off the street, she or he will not be turned away. Rather, she or he will be offered refreshment and included in the general celebration; or, the host may prepare a plate of takeaway food if that is the guest's preference. To turn away a stranger would be considered a sin. The *walima*, therefore, serves as an example of generosity and, equally as important, promotes the social and/or religious status of the host or hostess.

---

4 To a large number of Iranian nationalists, this recent phase of Iranian history is referred to as 'the second Arab invasion'. The first Arab invasion occurred when Islam was introduced to Iran and superseded Zoroastrianism.

5 Every day in the Islamic Republic of Iran, citizens are reminded of Ayatollah Khomeyni's legacy through a variety of media, such as videotapes, print media and quotations from his numerous sermons.

Figure 1 Sofrih Abolfazl, Muharram, Shiraz© Flaskerud 2002

Figure 2 Sofrih Abolfazl, Muharram, Shiraz© Flaskerud 2002

Cultural and religious significance of food

Scholarly research exploring the ritual significance of food has gained attention in numerous fields of inquiry, including history, sociology, anthropology, geography, gender discourse, literature, political economy and philosophy (Roden 2000). In terms of religion, food has played a key historic role. For example, in Caroline Walker Bynum's volume about (Christian) medieval women and their asceticism, she suggests, 'it is crucial to note that fasting, feasting, and feeding are merely aspects of the same phenomenon: the religious significance of food' (Bynum 1987, 227). In the fourteenth century, Ibn Qayyim Al-Jawziyya wrote *Medicine of the Prophet* about natural herbal and food remedies used for medicinal purposes (Al-Jawziyya 1998). Al-Jawziyya ties many of these restorative cures to *ahadith* of the Prophet Muhammad. Numerous 'Islamic' manuscripts have been written with specific curative food recipes, advising the reader on a desirable outcome if instructions are followed carefully. In these publications, a variety of foods, in combination with Quranic verses, are often used as edible talismans (e.g., Bahaei, n.d.).

Interest in the subject of food – as well as inquiry into the fields of literature addressing Islamic and Arab culinary arts specifically – is ever expanding. Eating and cooking are requisite human activities that reveal much about life and society. The Muslim attitude toward food is basically one of common sense: food is to be used for maintaining good health. Nutritious meals are, therefore, a necessity, and, most importantly, one should eat to live, rather than live only for the joy of eating. Feeding the poor is considered a *sadaqah*, or act of charity, which brings blessing to both donor and recipient. The Quran (7:31) warns against self-indulgence and asserts that the pious Muslim must try to obtain the highest quality food possible (18:18). Believers are also urged to 'eat of the wholesome things with which we have provided you and give thanks to God, if it is Him you worship' (2:172). Thus, the act of eating is itself a way of honouring God.

Along these lines, Javanese Muslims perceive food as a source of blessing and also a religious duty: 'Kejawen Muslims take pains to invite poor people to *slametan*, or at least send them some of the food' (Woodward 1988, 63; see also Muhaimin 1995). One of the practices of *slametan*,[6] in addition to prayers (*donga* or *du'a*), is *sidikah* (*sadaqa* or giving alms) on certain important occasions. *Sidikah* in the form of distributing food among the needy is a common practice. Santri Muslims of Java believe that dates and other food items from Arabia, such as coffee, are best for the *slametan* rituals because they are from the Prophet Muhammad's homeland. This belief already sets such food items apart in terms of religious importance.

From personal experience, I have noted that dates are the preferred food for breaking fasts among Muslims everywhere in the world, as this practice follows the tradition of the Prophet. Dates are served as ritual food in *sofrihs* and *walimas*; they are also the preferred offering of Shii Muslims, who distribute this food to the bereaved while visiting cemeteries. This particular act of food distribution is perceived as a *baraka* (God's blessing) and is considered an act of piety for all participants, including the deceased. Before consuming the food, the bereaved individual will recite a *fatiha* (first chap-

---

6 'The word *slamet* is borrowed from Arabic *salamah*, meaning peace or safety. Other words akin to *slametan*, and in many cases used interchangeably, are *kajatan*, *syukuran* or *tasyakuran*, and *sedekahan*, each of which is also borrowed from Arabic, respectively, from the word *hajah* (pl. hajat) meaning a need, *syukr* meaning thanking, *tasyakur* meaning to thank, and *sadaqah*, meaning to give alms or something to others'. Ibid. [because two sources are mentioned in the previous note, specify the source here]

ter of the Quran) for the blessing of the soul of the deceased person; thus the blessings multiply exponentially depending on the number of people participating in this graveside ritual.

For most Muslims, feeding the poor is understood as a religious duty and is considered a blessing. In mosques and other religious gathering places, sermons remind Muslims that feeding the poor is one of the most basic Islamic duties. The act of almsgiving is encouraged not only on special holy days but also throughout the entire year.

Muslims are also bound to certain dietary regulations, per Quranic and *hadith* instruction. The Quran (V: 4) speaks of forbidden foods for Muslim believers to avoid in their daily lives:

Forbidden to you (for food) are: dead meat, blood, the flesh of swine, and that on which hath been invoked the name of other than God. That which hath been killed by strangling, or by a violent blow, or by a headlong fall, or by being gored to death; That which hath been (partly) eaten by a wild animal, Unless ye are able to slaughter it (in due form), that which is sacrificed on stone (altars); (Forbidden) also is the division (of meat) by raffling with arrows: that is impiety (Ali 1983, 239–40.).

Muslims are allowed to partake of food from non-Muslims if those non-Muslims are people of the Book – namely, Christians and Jews[7]; 'the Quran indicates that the food of those who received the Scriptures is lawful [*halal*] for you, and your food is lawful for them' (Sakr 1971, 125; see also 'Dietary rules' 1995; Waines 2000). Hospitality is an especially important Muslim tradition, and food offerings play a key role.

Among Muslims, lavishing attention on one's guests is not a discretionary option, nor merely a matter of common courtesy – it is akin to a religious injunction. The Prophet Muhammad appears in many traditions (*hadith*) urging the faithful to be generous and hospitable to their guests, lest they attract God's wrath and jeopardise their chances of salvation (Rodriguez-Manas 2000, 59).

---

[7] Although Islam does not require a Muslim to abstain from eating or receiving food from Jews or Christians, Iranian cultural taboo prevents Muslims from receiving food from these sources. Perhaps this attitude is more directly related to the *haram/halal* concept regarding the specific type of meat consumed or the way an animal is slaughtered.

Muslim festivals and food

One of the most significant Muslim celebrations associated with food is the feast of sacrifice, or Eid al-adha (feast of sacrifice), occurring on the tenth day of the last month (Dhil-Hijja) of the lunar calendar. Those who are able to journey to Mecca on pilgrimage are requested to sacrifice an animal as a reminder of the great sacrifice of the Prophet Abraham. Likewise, those who are unable to go to Mecca but have the financial means to sacrifice an animal will do so to celebrate the occasion. Sheep, goats, cows or even camels may be used and eaten as sacrificial animals. Whoever purchases the animal, along with his family, must distribute a large portion of meat to feed the poor. Another festival that Muslims associate with food is *'Ashura* (the tenth of Muharram), honouring the martyrdom of Imam Hoseyn. The meat of sacrificial animals is also used in this observance. The consumption of food and drink at this celebration is considered a holy act filled with *baraka* (God's blessings). To distribute or partake in such meals is also believed to be an act of *savab* (good deed).

Ritual meals are popular in Muslim cultures around the world. However, in the practice of *slametan* of the *kanduri* (in Malay culture) an Indo-Persian practice is especially noted. The etymology of *kanduri* is complex. It is a Persian term, the literal meaning of which is 'tablecloth', and it is used in *Shafiite*[8] legal texts to refer to feasts held in honour of the Prophet Muhammad, the saints and souls of the dead. In the Malay language, the literal meaning of *kanduri* is 'a table for feasts' and, by extension, the feast itself. It is derived from the Persian word '*kundur*' (incense), which always accompanies food offerings.[9] In Muslim popular culture it is commonly believed that consumption of such meals prevents illness, as the meals has a magical or healing quality.

---

8 The *Shafiite* school of law traces its teaching to Muhammad ibn Idris al-Shafii. This particular tradition is prevalent in Indonesia and some parts of the Middle East. The *Shafiites* took the lead in developing *usul al-fiqh* (legal theory); the other schools except for the *Hanafites* use a system of *usul al-fiqh* similar to that of the *Shafiites*.
http://faculty-staff.ou.edu/V/David.R.Vishanoff-1/I-terms/madhhabs.htm (accessed 17 March 17 2009).

9 Woodward 1988, p. 64. Also see 'Kanduri [India] (1986.53)', October 2006, *Heilbrunn Timeline of Art History*, The Metropolitan Museum of Art, New York. http://www.metmuseum.org/TOAH/ho/11/ssa/ho_1986.53.htm

Another festive occasion that centres on food as ritual is the celebration of the Prophet's birth, *mawlidu n-nabiyyi* (or simply *mowludi*).This festival is celebrated in the third month of the Islamic calendar, Rabi'al-awal. As part of this celebration, families sacrifice an animal and distribute the meat among family members, friends and the poor. However, compared to the Eid al-adha or Eid al-feter (Muslim new year), this celebration is relatively small in scope (Tapper and Tapper 1986).

In Iran a number of celebrations rooted in Shii religious tradition include the preparation of a rich, sweet rice pudding flavoured with saffron. This pudding, known as *sholih zard,* is prepared for a variety of occasions. One of these occasions occurs during the month of Muharram, when the martyrdom of Imam Hoseyn is commemorated. *Sholih zard* is also prepared for the *mawlidu n-nabiyyi* in honour of the Prophet, or during those mourning days honouring a deceased loved one. After preparation, this sweet dish is distributed among neighbours, family members and friends and may also be sent to mosques, hospitals and orphanages. In addition to *sholih zard,* there are several *ash,* or stews, that can be prepared and distributed among friends and neighbours, or sent to mosques for distribution, when a person is looking forward to a favourable outcome or to honour a wish – this form of food, *ash- i nazri* (votive stew), can be prepared at anytime within any season and does not require any particular *sofrih.*

During the Muharram of 2009 (December 2008–January 2009), I was in Iran for five weeks of research. I witnessed and attended a number of gatherings in various homes (open to the public), where sermons included stories about the martyrdom of Imam Hoseyn and the courage of the Youth of Karbala (Abolfazl); the ceremony ended with the distribution of food, packed in disposable dishes and taken away by the guests. In the city of Yazd, I heard comments by women attending sermons and preparing to receive *nazri* food. These comments included, '*Ghazay-i Sofrihy-i Imam Hosyn shafa bakhash ast*' (food from the *sofrih* of Imam Hoseyn has healing qualities) and '*Didi ghazay-i Sofrihy-i Imam Hosyn chighadar khushmazih ast*?' (Have you noted how delicious the food from the *sofrih* of Imam Hoseyn is?). In Tehran on the ninth (*Tasu'a*) and eleventh days of Muharram, I decided to visit Imamzadeh Salih's shrine in Tajrish (located in northern Tehran). In the bazaar adjacent to this shrine, an organized religious group known as *hey'at* was serving freshly brewed tea to the public. I decided to take a cup of this hot beverage, known as *chay-i nazri* (votive tea), find a comfortable seat and observe the crowds of people. I sat next to an elderly woman sipping her tea, who seemed to be enjoying herself immensely. After finishing her beverage, she turned to me and said, '*Ghorbonash biram Imam Hoseyn, chighadar chay-i khoshmazihy-i darih*' (I love Imam Hoseyn; his tea tastes delicious).

Such comments demonstrate the strong and commonly held belief that any food or beverage prepared in honour of the Shii Imams will be extraordinarily potent, or will have curative properties – despite the fact that everyone knows perfectly well that the food is made from regular ingredients in regular kitchens. However, the deep belief in the power of votive meals runs through the very veins of Iranian people.

Sofrih as textile

In Iranian culture, *sofrih* plays a significant role and may be perceived through two distinct lenses. First, *sofrih* is identified as a textile, a piece of cloth that, as stated above, is the covering upon which a meal is served. There are also specific *sofrihs* used in bread-making. According to Parviz Tanavoli, 'Having two *sofrihs* is essential for every tribal and rural woman: one for making dough and the other for baking bread. When the woman sits by the oven, she places a *sofrih* for dough on one side of her and another *sofrih,* for bread, on the other side'(Tanavoli 2001, 17). This means that the entire dough eventually is used to prepare bread. While baking, the woman closes both *sofrihs* by wrapping the four corners of each, preventing its contents from drying out. Tanavoli also studied specific *sofrihs* for their designs, colours, weaves and functions.[10]

The type of *sofrih* shown here is a highly prized, expensive handcrafted product made in Kamou, a village in the region of Joshaghan, near the city of Kashan, which has a long history of weaving fine, exclusive Iranian carpets.

Sofrih: ritual and ceremony

The second type of *sofrih* I would like to discuss is a female-only event in which food plays a significant, sacred role. Iranian Muslim women wishing

10 Tanavoli 1998. The author has two such *sofrihs* in her personal collection; both are mentioned in this chapter.

for a beneficial outcome, even one that may seem almost impossible or miraculous, traditionally have turned to one or more forms of *sofrih* in order to fulfil their wishes. The hostess of a *sofrih* will offer a prayer for a specific outcome or event. She will vow that if her prayer is answered, she will then host another *sofrih* in gratitude, or contribute ingredients to a *sofrih* hosted by another woman. Guests at a *sofrih* can pray for whatever they choose and will likewise vow that if they receive that for which they pray, they will host or contribute to a *sofrih*. Thus, one *sofrih* may spawn another. Many women have a favourite *sofrih*; one might repeatedly or annually host a *sofrih* to honour a saint or holy person to whom she is especially devoted. Guests at a *sofrih* honouring a particular holy person often will vow that, if their wishes are granted, they will host another *sofrih* in honour of the same holy person. Men are not participants in this ritual; only women sponsor, produce and attend these votive meals. As such, the *sofrih* fulfils a psychological need to mingle and share life experiences among women of similar social status – and particularly among Muslim women who hold a similar religious belief in the power of Shii Imams.

For each *sofrih*, careful attention is paid to correct preparations. The time of day or month in which the *sofrih* is held; the manner in which the food is prepared, displayed and partaken; the ingredients; the types of utensils and dishes used for preparation and serving; even the site where food is prepared – all are symbolically significant. Paying close attention to these details is believed to bring a positive outcome toward the fulfilment of a vow, or *nazr*. In the following sections, I discuss two of the most popular types of *sofrihs* celebrated by Iranian Shii women.

Sofrihy-i Umm al-Banin, the mother of Abolfazl

It is believed that *Sofrihy-i Umm al-Banin* is potent for a variety of wishes, including regaining health, repaying debts and safe travel. Central to this *sofrih* is the ritual food offering, or *ghazay-i nazri*, of a special form of stew known as *ash-i amaj kumaj*. Women who have a child or husband in prison strongly believe in the power of this stew, prepared to honour Umm al-Banin, mother of Abolfazl. This belief is rooted in symbolism based on the Tragedy of Karbala. In that battle, Abolfazl was surrounded by the enemy's army, trapped and effectively cut off from the outside world. Two groups of people are forbidden to eat *ash-i amaj kumaj*: men and pregnant women. It is believed that any man who eats this stew will eventually be imprisoned. If a pregnant woman who is expecting a boy eats the stew, that male child will be jailed as an adult (Mirnia 1990, 192–95).

Abolfazl, one of the martyrs of Karbala, is also known as Abolfazl al-Abbas. Abolfazl accompanied his paternal uncle, Imam Hoseyn, the son of Imam 'Ali, better known to Shiis as Siyied al-Shohada (Master of Martyrs), from Medina to Karbala. Abolfazl joined the ranks of Hoseyn, fighting against Yazid's army during the Battle of Karbala. According to historical documents, Abolfazl was killed by Abdullah ibn Aqaba in Karbala. In the Shii tradition, Abolfazl is also known as Qamar-i Bani Hashem, or the Moon of the Hashemi people, the tribe of the Prophet Muhammad. In popular Shii culture, seeking help from Abolfazl begins by invoking his name, simply referring to him as *Ya Abbas*.

People believe that honouring Abolfazl with a *sofrih* is a remedy to ward off danger, misfortune or sickness (Mirnia 1990, 207). This is one of the most common and often one of the most elaborate of *sofrihs*. The required food items are quite simple: bread, yogurt and fresh herbs. Depending on the status of the host, there could be a variety of other cooked and uncooked foods present at the table, including *adas polo* (cooked lentils and rice), *ash* (a thick vegetable soup or stew), and *sholih zard* (saffron-flavoured sweet rice, similar to pudding).

What do the *walima* and *sofrih* share in common? Essentially, both focus on the importance of community, sharing and acknowledging the blessing inherent in bountiful food, as well as engaging in prayer on behalf of self and other. In both contexts, prayers are offered hierarchically: first to God, then to the *Chahardah Ma'sum*, or fourteen Infallible Ones (this includes the Prophet, his daughter Fatima and the twelve Shii Imams). Prayer may also be offered for people who are ill or in debt; for women unable to conceive a child or who have children or relatives in prison; or for those in any other critical situation. The host(ess) of the *walima* and *sofrih* will, in fact, ask the assembled guests to offer names of individuals, living or deceased, to be included in prayer. It should be noted that the *sofrih* is a thorny issue with some orthodox clerics, many of whom oppose such gatherings. They contend that these events cannot be considered valid forms of religious practice. At times, clerics have referred to *sofrihs* as female gossip groups or frivolous social parties. Some clerics even hold the extreme view that hosting and attending *sofrihs* is irreligious. Regardless of how the *sofrih* is viewed by religious authorities, it remains a strong cultural/religious tradition and is a special part of a Shii woman's religious life.

Walima as public relations event

Before embarking on the Hajj journey, pilgrims customarily bid farewell to friends and ask forgiveness for any past wrongdoings, intentional or unintentional. In addition, pilgrims request blessings and good wishes for a successful journey to Mecca, after which they are honoured with the titles *haji* and *hajia*.

It is also customary for a pilgrim to carry with her or him a list of names of loved ones, both alive and deceased. The pilgrim will recite prayers for these beloved family members and friends, remembering them during this most holy journey. It is said that all *du'as* (prayers) made during the Hajj trip will be answered. Believing in the power of *du'a*, many individuals, at some point during their visits to the Masjid al-Haram, will seek Allah's help and blessing, not only for themselves but also for those they left behind. Thus, the pious will share the spiritual benefits and experiences of Hajj with many people who are not physically present or who are no longer living. Pilgrims returning from Mecca arrive home with a new sense of religious awareness. The ritual and spiritual experiences of Hajj offer opportunities for a new approach to life when one returns. Because Hajj entitles a person to a new and elevated religious status, there is a risk that some 'believers' will use this status to boast, to promote themselves and to seek public and private advantage. Public announcements on the part of returning *hajis*, which are often extravagant and ostentatious, have become commonplace.

In effect, global consumerism has largely succeeded in commodifying religion and religious practice; Muslims are no exception. Many pilgrims returning from Hajj ensure that their new social and religious status is publicized in a number of ways, including the use of huge banners displayed to the public announcing *hajis'* and *hajias'* safe return from visiting the *ka'ba*, referred to in Iranian culture as *khanihy-i khoda* (God's House). Friends and family members compete with one another to display the biggest and best banners. Whether hanging from the outer walls of a residence or in front of public restaurants or catering sites, these banners announce in large letters the neighbourhood's new *haji agha* (Mr. *haji*) or *hajia khanom* (Mrs. *hajia*).

Each *walima* begins with the *niyah* (statement of intent). This is a welcoming speech given by the host to welcome attendees and let them know the purpose of the *walima.* Frequently, the host will apologize in advance for the inadequacy of the food or space, requisite protocol in Persian culture. This 'apology' is meant to inform guests that their host feels obliged (culturally and religiously) to provide them with the best and most excellent entertainment and refreshments. In the Persian language, there are multiple references to the status of the guest and the responsibility of the host, including *mihman aziz-i khodast* (the guest is dear to God), *mihman habib-i khodast* (the guest is a friend of God), or *ghadam-i mihman ruy-i chishm* (which literally translates as 'the steps [feet] of the guest upon one's eyes' – a very humble way of stating that guests are most welcome). Such common proverbs afford guests an elevated status. The act of entertaining one's guest becomes, therefore, almost a holy ritual or sacred act.

The *walima niyah* is carefully crafted. Indeed, here is a rare opportunity for the host to establish a more prestigious status in the community through the public display of his piety and devotion to God. The host may even seize on this opportunity to suggest a link with the Prophet himself, given that the Prophet also officiated at ritual meals. The host will also praise Allah for giving him the means and health to complete the obligatory trip to Mecca. The host may offer blessings to the Prophet, his household and the Shii imams, along with a request that guests join in this blessing.

Walimas given to honour individuals who have returned from Hajj usually include a number of elaborate dishes prepared by caterers, professional chefs or family members. These individuals work for days in advance to prepare sumptuous meals, using only the finest, freshest ingredients. If, for example, one were to serve leftovers or pre-cooked food from a can to guests at a *walima*, it would be considered unacceptable or insulting.

All of the extreme preparation efforts and lavish expenditures on food that a *walima* requires stand in direct contrast to many *ahadith.* Hosting a lavish Hajj banquet contradicts some of the Prophet's most important spiritual teachings about food. For example, the Prophet suggests that the experience of hunger is necessary to develop compassion for those who are poor or less fortunate. In fact, obligatory fasting during the month of Ramadan is directly linked to this spiritual lesson: the necessity of identifying more readily with those in need. Among the *ahadith* attributed to food and lifestyle are the Prophet's warnings about the experience of gluttony: the food of two will be enough to feed three people, and the food of three suffices for four. In essence, the holiest man in Islam clearly set boundaries for indulging in food. While we know that the Prophet enjoyed dates, we are also taught that he insisted that a single date would be sufficient to satisfy a man's hunger. It would seem that the Prophet intended to warn believers against the temptation of gluttony.

Similarly, the philosophy of Hajj instructs the pilgrim to detach from material goods and practices in order to focus on the richness of spiritual understanding. Unfortunately, *walimas* often undermine and contradict this original intention by encouraging gift-giving by the host and by the guests. Instead of keeping the focus on spiritual attainment, the pilgrim must spend precious Hajj hours milling around shopping malls, searching for 'party favours' – almost all of which are manufactured in non-Muslim lands, such as China. The anxiety connected with pleasing future *walima* guests often spoils the spirit of Hajj, replacing the rare opportunity for transcendence with worldly concerns regarding social status, material wealth and ostentatious show. Although religious scholars have cautioned *hajis* against these elaborate, show-off practices, this spectacle continues to take place throughout Iran.

Concluding remarks

Whether as a symbol of hospitality or a marker of ethnic identity and regional preference, food has always conveyed powerful social and cultural messages. Numerous scholars, such as Sabry Hafez (Hafez 2000), have explored this symbolic, age-old aspect of food. In both Arab and Persian cultures, one's gratitude to Allah for food received and one's generosity in sharing food with others combine to define, in part, what it means to be a pious Muslim.

As in all other cultures, food in Iran is completely intertwined with social and religious customs. Both the *sofrih* and *walima* shed thought-provoking light on the role of food in contemporary Iranian Shii rituals and celebrations.

Bibliography

Ali, Y. 1983. *The Holy Quran: Text, Translation and Commentary*. Bentwood: Amana Corporation.

Al-Jawziyya, I. Q. 1998. *Medicine of the Prophet* (trans.) P. Johnstone. Cambridge: The Islamic Texts Society.

Bahaei, S. n.d. *Majmu'h Ulumi Gharibih: Kashkuli Shaykh-i Bahayi*. Tehran: Offset Publisher.

Bynum, C. W. 1987. *Holy Feast and Holy Fast: The Religious Significance of Food to Medieval Women*. Berkeley: University of California Press.

Dehkhoda, A. 1994. *Loghatname (Encyclopedic Dictionary)*. Tehran: Tehran University Publication.

'Dietary Rules'. 1995. *The Oxford Encyclopedia of the Modern Islamic World*, 375–77. New York: New York University Press.

Hafez, S. 2000. 'Food as a semiotic code in Arabic literature'. In *A Taste of Thyme: Culinary Cultures of the Middle East* (eds) S. Zobeideh and R. Tapper, 257–80. New York: Tauris.

Mirnia, S. A. 1990. *Farhangi Mardum*. Tehran: Nashr-i Parsa.

Muhaimin, A.G. 1995. *The Islamic Traditions of Cirebon Ibadat and Adat among Javanese Muslims*. Canberra: ANU E Press, The Australian National University.

Roden, C. 2000. 'Foreword'. In *A Taste of Thyme: Culinary Cultures of the Middle East* (eds) S. Zobeideh and R. Tapper, vii_ix. New York: Tauris.

Rodriguez-Manas, F. 2000. 'Charity and deceit: the practice of the *it'am al-ta'am* in Moroccan Sufism'. *Studia Islamica* 91: 59–90.

Sakr, A. H. 1971. 'Dietary regulations and food habits of Muslims'. *Journal of the American Dietetic Association* 58: 123–26.

Shirazi, F. 2005. 'The *Sofrih*: comfort and community among women in Iran Sofrih'. *Iranian Studies* 38, no. 2: 293–309.

Tanavoli, P.1998. *Sofrih hay-i Kamou*. Tehran: Farhangsara.

———. 2001. *Rustic and Tribal Weaves from Varamin*. Tehran: Aban Printing House.

Tapper, R., and N. Tapper. 1986. 'Eat This, It'll Do You a Power of Good: Food and Commensality among Durrani Pashtuns'. In *American Ethnologist* 13, no. 1: 63–80.

Waines, D. 2000. 'Muslim piety and food of the gods'. *Al-Qantara, Revista De Estudios Arabes* XXI, fasc. 2: 411–24.

Woodward, M. R. 1988. 'The slametan: textual knowledge and ritual performance in central Javanese Islam'. *History of Religions* 28, no. 1: 54–89.

Gageriveh, Bakhtiari women's lamentations: between self-suffering and tribal identity

Pedram Khosronejad

Introduction

Until recently, most anthropological and ethnographic discourses on death in relation to Muslim communities have tended to ignore cultural practices and lived experiences characterized by 'improvisation, subjectivity and particularity'.[1] Instead, they concentrate on formality, externality and generality. Therefore, aside from being inhumane, the result is superficial social analyses. Generally speaking, most ethnographic studies consider death under the rubric of 'ritual' rather than 'bereavement'; the subtitles of many books on death make the emphasis on ritual explicit. Huntington and Metcalf's *Celebrations of Death* is subtitled *The Anthropology of Mortuary Ritual*,[2] and Douglas's *Death in Murelaga* is subtitled *Funerary Ritual in a Spanish Basque Village*.[3] In these works, ritual is defined by its formality and routine; it is virtually a program for action, more like a recipe or book of etiquette rather than an actual event or a human process. Most ethnographic descriptions thus preserve a sense of programmed unfolding which enables the topic of analysis to remain mourning rites rather than bereavement.[4]

Even today, most ethnographers write more as witnesses to visual spectacles than as people who converse with mourners and participate in death ceremonies. They notice not what the bereaved say about their experiences but externally observable differences in mourning behaviour by members of

1 Rosaldo 2005.
2 Huntington and Metcalf 1991.
3 Douglas 1969.
4 Rosaldo 2005, 27.

different social categories. Therefore, in sum, ethnographic writing concentrates on routine expressions of grief and programmed ways of handling the corpse immediately after death. In all cases, the ethnographer is a spectator, witnessing events from the outside and not asking people about their subjective experiences.[5] Further, most ethnographic accounts see grief in partial and mechanistic ways and even remain sceptical about the emotional experience of grieving. Rosaldo argues that such ethnographic accounts maintain that the work of mourning occurs only in connection to formal rituals.[6] Arguably, the problem with ethnographic writing on death resides not only in distanced normalizing discourse but also in an excessive reliance on a metaphoric rather than metonymic analysis of culture in general and ritual in particular.[7]

The problem, as some anthropologists suggest, is that one cannot conflate the study of death and the study of death ritual,[8] 'yet these are interconnected in cultural and social life and must therefore be connected in analysis in order to understand, for example, the problem of the women's weeping and the dissenting local interpretations of it'.[9] Therefore, most of the anthropological approaches to death that confine the analysis of bereavement to ritual contexts have come under heavy criticism in recent years.[10] It is claimed that structuralist and objectivist analyses that vaporize the study of bounded events and the perspective of the detached observer marginalise the study of grief.[11] Transcending this theoretically infertile ground requires reflexive involvement on the part of the anthropologist and the opening up of new areas of sociality to serious analytical scrutiny: what Rosaldo calls the 'informal settings of everyday life'.[12]

However, contextually defined, 'formal' or 'informal', 'ritual' or 'secular', death and bereavement are examples of human suffering that challenge the discipline's theoretical biases toward holism, integration and observer detachment, as recently discussed by Hastrup.[13]Among other anthropolog-

---

5 Rosaldo 2005, 429.
6 Ibid., 429.
7 Ibid., 425.
8 Huntington and Metcalf 1991, 5; Rosaldo 2005, 194.
9 Rasmussen 2000, 395.
10 Rosaldo 2005; Seremetakis 1991.
11 Rosaldo 2005, 185–9.
12 Ibid., 187.
13 Hastrup 1993, 728.

ical studies of death rituals, Van Gennep made a critical contribution by interpreting mortuary rituals as one of many related rites of passage. In his words, 'the life of an individual in any society is a series of passages from one age to another and from one occupation to another'.[14] Surely one of the most prominent aspects of death is its potential for intense emotional impact on the survivors. The reasons are as numerous as they are obvious: the simple but often searing fact of separation from a loved one; the realization that he or she will no longer enjoy the fruits of life; and the suddenness with which death can strike.[15]

The initial denial of a loved one's death and, more often, a numbing depression after the death, are prominent elements of mourning, particularly in its early stages. Feelings and images of abandonment, isolation and self-absorption, disintegration and despair preoccupy survivors as they face the traumatic event that calls into question their own continued existence.[16]

As in other monotheistic faiths, in Islamic imagery death, afterlife and the hereafter play prominent roles. For the believer, the present world is a prison, whereas the tomb is a fortress that gives way to the Garden: Paradise. For the unbeliever, the present world is the Garden, whereas the tomb is his prison, which gives way to the Fire: Hell. Yet there have never been anchored convictions or beliefs in Islam regarding death, afterlife and the hereafter. No one escapes death, and theoretically all Muslims should be buried in accordance with specific rites.

In addition to the beliefs about death and the hereafter stated above, the development of an intense mortuary cult in Iran has been reinforced by the fact that eleven of the twelve Shiite Imams suffered a violent death and thus are considered martyrs, whose intercession on behalf of believers was taken for granted. Therefore, the deeply rooted sense of suffering and public grieving over the fate of the Imams is typical of the main branches of Shiism in modern Iran. This is why some modern theologians have tried to purge Shiism of some of the elements associated with visitation rites and with the sentiment of suffering.[17]

As is the case for many societies, in Iran religious beliefs have a strong influence on the conceptualization of death and its associated practices. Be-

---

[14] Van Gennep 1960.

[15] Huntington and 1991, 42.

[16] Homerin 1990, 555.

[17] For more information, see: Thurfjell 2006.

cause Iran is officially a Shiite community, resurrection is also a recurring theme. Iranian society is made up of thinking individuals, not merely unquestioning 'machines' blindly following the tenets of their religion, and funerary traditions in Iran are the product of these individuals and of society as a whole. They are born from a desire for commemoration in order to assuage grief, to reinforce social position in death as in life, to achieve piety and to gain identity.[18]

Bereavement ceremonies among Bakhtiari

Death and funerary rituals also have a special significance among Bakhtiari, one of the primary groups of pastoral nomads in modern Iran,[19] The death of a clan or family member is not merely a biological event mourned by the deceased's relatives. Rather, the death evokes the clan's moral, and the tribe's social, obligations, which are expressed through religiously determined funeral practices and bereavement ceremonies. The number as well as the scale of the Bakhtiari nomads' funerary ceremonies varies according to the sex, age, sociopolitical status and cause of death of the deceased: both the depth of the mourners' shock and the degree of drama that characterizes the subsequent events depend on the age and identity of the departed as well as the circumstances of the death.

My long-term field observations and my participation in several funeral ceremonies among the Bakhtiari nomads reveal that funeral ceremonies and interment rituals are long and deeply painful processes through which society gradually confronts the loss of a loved one. Close relatives keep the loved one company during his or her final days, care for the corpse, assume the social status of mourners and display their grief.[20] The ceremony begins at the moment of death and may last for weeks or even a year.[21] Surviv-

---

18 For more information, watch: Mortezayi 2006.

19 The Bakhtiari are among the important nomadic tribal groups that have had a long connection with and influence on the political life of Iran during the last three centuries. They are a semi-nomadic people, living in the southwest of the Bakhtiari Mountains and migrating twice a year between their winter and summer pastures, leaving in spring and returning in autumn. They are Muslims of the Imamate (Twelver) branch of Shiism· For more information, see: Khosronejad 2013.

20 For more information, watch: Khosronejad 2004.

21 Because of massive urbanism and the influence of urban clerics, today a large part of

Figure 1: Funeral of A Jafar Quli Rustami, Kuhrang; Chahar Mahal va Bakhtiari, Iran © CNRS Mission, Khosronejad 2004

Figure 2: Interview with A Quli the best cavalier of A Jafar Quli Rustami, Kuhrang; Chahar Mahal va Bakhtiari, Iran © CNRS Mission, Khosronejad 2004

Bakhtiari traditional funerary ceremonies are banned by the local governor in Lali Plain of Khuzestan.

ing relatives want to both break and prolong their relationships with the deceased; over time, the reality of the person's death is confirmed, and former attachments are slowly joined to consoling substitutes, including the memory and idealized image of the dead.

What is much more significant among Bakhtiari funeral rituals is that, in the funeral ceremonies of great men and chiefs, we can still observe old traditions that do not exist in other parts of Iran.[22] For example, the men, in traditional dress (*chuqa*), bring out their firearms and shout in the memory of their chief. The *toshmal* (traditional musicians) play the *chapi* (left music), the traditional funeral music of the Bakhtiari; the professional male lamenters recite the *sorud* and the *Shahnameh* (The Epic of Kings).[23] A man close to the deceased, dressed traditionally, leads a white mare that is decorated with coloured ribbons and the arms of the deceased around his *Mafeh-gah* (a special cubic memorial structure).[24]

Figure 3: Funeral of A Jafar Quli Rustami, Kuhrang; Chahar Mahal va Bakhtiari, Iran © CNRS Mission, Khosronejad 2004

22 For more information, watch Khosronejad: 2004.

23 For more information, see: Khosronejad 2006; and Khosronejad 2011.

24 For more information on this ritual, watch: Khosronejad 2004.

Figure 4: Funeral of A Jafar Quli Rustami, Kuhrang; Chahar Mahal va Bakhtiari, Iran © CNRS Mission, Khosronejad 2004

Certainly, among the Bakhtiari nomads one of the most important elements of such funeral ceremonies is the traditional lamentations of women. The responses to death among the Bakhtiari are gendered, and lamenting, as in other nomadic societies in Iran, is primarily women's activity.[25] In this context, laments and a repertoire of conventional nonverbal practices of Bakhtiari grief and grieving, which include weeping, tearing, screaming, sobbing and scratching the face, all belong to the confined time and place of the women's lamentation ritual, traditionally named *Gageriveh*.

25 It is important to note that, since the Iranian revolution of 1978, we can see increasing performances of professional male lamenters in public ceremonies.

Figure 5: Funeral of A Jafar Quli Rustami, Kuhrang; Chahar Mahal va Bakhtiari, Iran © CNRS Mission, Khosronejad 2004

Figure 6: Funeral of A Jafar Quli Rustami, Kuhrang; Chahar Mahal va Bakhtiari, Iran © CNRS Mission, Khosronejad 2004

Gageriveh's etymology and function

From the eighteenth century on, travellers' accounts, rare histories, folklore collections, community studies of the Bakhtiari and external observers have agreed on the centrality of mortuary rituals in the region and on the pivotal role that women play in them.[26] The ballads and hymns that the women sing and recite in lamenting those dear to them, especially at ceremonies for great men (*khan*[27], *kalantar*[28], *shekalu*[29]), have maintained an important sociopolitical and symbolic significance for the Bakhtiari. It can be concluded from my interviews and ethnographic field observations conducted with the Bakhtiari, as well as the words of the *Gageriveh,* that such rituals were originally held exclusively for the great men of the tribe who had shown outstanding courage and bravery or had enjoyed an impressive social status. Today, however, they are held for men, women and even children.

Among the Bakhtiari, *Gageriveh* is the name given to the song sung by a choir of tribal women to mourn a death among their beloved. In most cases, *Gageriveh* is a private oral ritual that allows women and their female audience to raise questions of life and death and to express their sorrow in a shared communal act. "'They remind the bereaved that while death has occurred, annihilation has not."[30] The word *Gageriveh* is used among the Bakhtiari with different pronunciations and meanings: *Gah Gerive* – the time of weeping; *Gu Gerive* – say and weep; *Gow Gerive* – weep, brother; *Gor Gerive* – even the wolves weep in sadness; and *Gav Gerive* – even the bulls weep in sadness. *Gerive*, the common element, means 'weeping, crying and sobbing'. Perhaps the closest pronunciation to the original is *Gu Gerive*, combining *gooy*, meaning 'say, talk, recite', and *Gerive*, meaning 'sobbing, tearing', to imply the act of talking about the deceased, weeping and crying in his memory.

Gageriveh is part of a longstanding oral tradition in which the literary concept of one authentic or correct version of a song does not exist. These traditional laments are composed, performed and transmitted orally.[31]

---

26 For more information, see: Khosronejad 2006.

27 Literally, 'chief'.

28 Literally, 'sheriff'.

29 Literally, 'a hunter'.

30 Lifton 1983, 3.

31 For more information, see: Khosronejad 2006; Khosronejad 2011; and Khosronejad 2013.

Bakhtiari women are not in any sense professional mourners. They are unpaid, and in most cases they have become good singers and have learned many *Gageriveh* rituals? because they have had much experience of death and funeral ceremonies. Contrary to countries (Greece, for example) in which – due to the rapid rate of urbanisation and modernisation – most younger women do not know the laments, and/or do not approve of them, young Bakhtiari women and even young girls can recite different versions of *Gageriveh*. Among the Bakhtiari, although several women have the ability to compose *Gageriveh*, the vast majority of laments sung are well known to most women. In such cases the variations involve the complexity and the degree of elaboration with which traditional themes are presented. The degree to which each performance is an original creation or composition varies greatly from one region to another – and, within any region, from one performer to another.

The *Gageriveh* ritual is carried out exclusively by women in a separate space from that of men. The older female family members, as the 'owners of the death', sit waiting for the guests. The female guests announce their arrival with particular screams (*kikovak*)[32] while scratching their faces and tearing their hair. Then they enter the women's place that is prepared for them under the tent or in the women's room.

Close female relatives of the deceased (grandchildren, nieces, cousins) rise, take the hands of the arriving women (*dast-giri*)[33] as a token of accepting their sympathy, and undo their mourning scarves (*chador bazkardan*), which have been tied behind their necks.[34] Then one older female leads a *Gageriveh,* and the others answer her in chorus.[35] Generally, in the beginning of the ceremon, singing is led by women who are less directly touched by the death. Wives, daughters, mothers and sisters of the deceased, those who are most moved by his death, do not usually lead the singing of laments, because they are too overcome by grief and sadness. They spend much of their time tearing, sobbing, and calling out to the deceased. Later, priority is customarily accorded to close female agnates, but more distant kin, co-villagers and even women who are not related to the deceased can make claims of precedence, particularly if they are known

32 A local female scream that is a signal of arrival at the funeral ceremony.

33 Literally, 'taking hands'.

34 A sign of welcoming and respect.

35 For more information, watch: Khosronejad 2004.

Figure 7: Funeral of one of the local chiefs of Chengayi tribe, Lali, Khuzestan, Iran© Khosronejad 1999

to be skilled lamenters. I think that often the women who lead the singing are themselves in mourning and, through their singing, they express their grief and sadness for their own beloveds. As has been mentioned, not every Bakhtiari woman who laments is a relative of the deceased. However, even in these cases kinship is stressed because the lamenter instead invokes the closest members of her own immediate family, clan or tribe who have died, usually a father, a brother, or a husband.

While performing *Gageriveh,* women may lose control. They often repeat certain words when deeply moved or in a trance, and the other women echo these words. While in this mental state, they have been known to scratch their faces, drawing blood with their fingernails, and to punch themselves in the belly and drum their chests with their fists; nearby women must hold their hands tightly to prevent them from hurting themselves.[36] After the singing of each verse of *Gageriveh*, there is a break during which women cry, sob or talk emotionally about the recent death and drink tea.

[36] For more information, watch: Khosronejad 2004.

Figure 8: Funeral of A Jafar Quli Rustami, Kuhrang; Chahar Mahal va Bakhtiari, Iran © CNRS Mission, Khosronejad 2004

The lyrics of the *Gageriveh* generally consist of an homage to a deceased male. Lyrics are passed orally from mothers to their daughters over several generations, beginning in early childhood. During the ceremony, the order of songs and hymns is determined by the social position and status of the deceased rather than by any fixed, inherent order. Generally speaking, the *Gageriveh* lyrics can be categorised into the following themes:

- the courage and bravery of the deceased;
- his hunting and shooting prowess;
- his social position;
- his husbandry;
- his kindness and generosity;
- his faith and religious fervour; and
- his wealth.

An important feature throughout the songs, as has been mentioned, is the name of the deceased, which should be mentioned in the lyrics and is

Figure 9: Funeral of A Jafar Quli Rustami, Kuhrang; Chahar Mahal va Bakhtiari, Iran © CNRS Mission, Khosronejad 2004

of course different in each ceremony. One should also note that the lyrics depend on the relationship between the singers and the deceased and hence differ, for example, between the mother and the daughter of the dead person.

Each time a *Gageriveh* is sung, the proper names, kinship terms and descriptive phrases that fit the circumstances of the deceased are inserted in the appropriate places. Finally, certain laments or themes are only appropriate for certain categories of people. A lament suitable for a young man who has died, for example, in a car accident would not be sung at the funeral of an old chief. All *Gageriveh* lyrics describe scenes that are very prominent in the traditional Bakhtiari way of living, although such scenes may no longer exist today. It should be mentioned that the nomadic way of life inevitably created certain responsibilities for the men of the tribe, which have become fixed in the society's mentality. Supervising the tribe's affairs, defending the women and children against wild animals, thieves and highwaymen, and taking care of the cattle were among these responsibilities, and today we can identify such scenes in the lyrics of *Gageriveh.* [37]

One popular scene among the Bakhtiari is the depiction of horseback riding, for example. In the past, the possession of a horse was a prerequisite for great men, all of whom were skilled rider warriors. Today, one can rarely find even one good horseman among the Bakhtiari, and the large herds of horses that once roamed the plains have long since disappeared. In many *Gageriveh* songs the saddle – made abroad and lined with leopard or sable – is mentioned, too, which demonstrates that this object was once important for the Bakhtiari.[38]

Other such scenes include hunting and hunters. Often, the ibex, or wild goat, appears symbolically in the lyrics and is hunted by the *shekalu* (deceased). The ibex is a fast and intelligent animal which only experienced hunters could catch, which is why, today, at the funeral ceremonies of chiefs and tribesmen, the head and horns of the ibex are put on the *Mafeh-gah.* Another *Gageriveh* depiction includes the wild lion, which symbolizes the bravery and valour of Bakhtiari men.[39] The yellow lion, whose habitat was *Zard Kuh* (yellow mountain), the highest and the most revered mountain in the *Kuhrang* (coloured mountain) region, is now extinct. The lion is very important to these nomads as a symbol of bravery – so important that, in the past, gravestones (*bard-e shir*) of great men were made in the form of a lion.[40] A further symbolic image is that of the mountain of *Zard Kuh* (*zardeh*) and its streams of yellow water (*ab-e zard*). According to the lyrics, the mountain embraces the deceased and thereby picks a beautiful flower from the garden.

Following my long periods of field research among Bakhtiari nomads, I propose that the image of burial and symbolic resurrection is an ancient and crucial theme, and that for them it is a means of keeping symbolic acts and memories alive. Also, based on my direct participation in funerals, I can confirm that for the Bakhtiari nomads, especially women, the loss of death is the movement of the self from the inside to the outside. This passage signifies the disorderly exposure of interiority. For Bakhtiari women, the passages of *Gageriveh* discourse in a symbolic movement toward sobbing

---

37 For more information, see: Khosronejad 2006.

38 I am presently working on a collection regarding the lyrics of Bakhtiari *Gageriveh.*

39 For more information, see: Khosronejad 2006.

40 For more information, see: ibid.

are a simulation of death, an expression of each lamenter's social death as a response to the personal loss she has recently experienced.

Among the Bakhtiari, especially women, it is perhaps the fact that death can come so suddenly that makes the experience so horrifying at the beginning. In focusing on the moment of discovery and the way in which death arrives, my field studies confirm that the narratives of *Gageriveh* capture the ways in which death turns life upside down. Every narrative includes some mention of how the person speaking, others whom the speaker and listener know in common, or those family members most concerned (e.g., the mother, sister or daughter of the deceased) learned of the death, along with remarks about his life and his manner among his family and his clan or tribe. This aspect of the narratives can be seen as providing commentary on the meaning of the death for the family as well as reflection on personal attachments.[41]

Also, my ethnographic observations demonstrate that, in *Gageriveh,* emphasis is placed on the transformation of clan or tribal memory into symbolic narrative. Therefore, in any anthropological research regarding death rituals, we should be sensitive to the concerns of narratology. This requires consideration of narrative structure and an ability to interpret tribal experiences as schematized images. Indeed, the transformation of memory into narrative loosens the ties of the original experience, like literary texts breaking free from the author's original inspiration.[42] *Gageriveh* lyrics and narrations demonstrate the extent to which the antiphonic construction of pain and mourning did not solely display a self-referential trajectory but was a process that intentionally intervened in the tribal institutional order, outside the Bakhtiari funerary ceremonies and death rituals.

Gageriveh's weeping and shedding tears

For a Bakhtiari woman, engaging in *Gageriveh's* weeping also serves as a mark of her changed social status. A Bakhtiari woman who weeps for her deceased husband, brother, relative or clan member thereby demonstrates that she, her family or her clan embody specific political and symbolic values associated with being a proper wife, mother and so forth. For example, a young Bakhtiari widow is an especially tragic figure, prematurely thrown

41 Abu-Lughod 1993, 197.

42 Khosronejad 2006.

into this social and ritual status. Older Bakhtiari women, however, gain respect and, at times, a far-flung reputation by participating in collective ceremonies of *Gageriveh's* weeping.

Further, during *Gageriveh* rituals, tears – whether actually shed, withheld or represented performatively, pictorially, or narratively – must be understood in terms of tribal moral values and perhaps social codes, as well as the aesthetics and politics of affective display. In such cases, as Ebersole remarks[43], we must concern ourselves with the cultural poetics of ritual and ritualized *Gageriveh's* weeping. I think that in the case of *Gageriveh*, more focus is on 'performative' tears, those shed in lamentation ceremonies proper or in ritualized social situations that perform sociopolitical work, as well as in the discursive activity that takes place around tears-as-signs. *Gageriveh's* ritual tears serve a 'variety of social purposes, including marking out social and hierarchical relationships at times, dissolving them at others, inviting or demanding specific social relationships, or protesting the abrogation of social and moral contracts'.[44]

After my fieldwork, I can confirm that some of the *Gageriveh's* ritual tears are shed out of grief, while others are shed out of 'respect' and 'courtesy'. Bakhtiari women's tears shed specifically while singing a *Gageriveh* publicly mark the breach of a moral contract, but they can also offer a critique of the oppressive aspects of their tribal and nomadic social system. *Gageriveh,* then, I propose, protests not only the personal suffering of the female singer but also the rules of hierarchy. I also consider *Gageriveh* a type of 'screaming of the dead'. Traditional *Gageriveh's* screaming, which invokes the passage of breath and sound from the inside to the outside, is also a metaphor of the disruptive and violent passage of Bakhtiari women from inside to outside – that is, to the domain of loss, separation, pain and death.

For Bakhtiari women who actively participate in *Gageriveh* sessions and the improvisation of lament poetry, *discoursed pain* and *discourse in pain* constitute truth. This is an antiphonic construction precisely because its expression is invested in prescribed contrastive modes of signification, such as poetic improvisation, prose monologues, ritual sobbing, screaming and iconographies of the body.[45] Therefore, I suggest that *Gageriveh*'s ritu-

43 Ebersole 2000, 213.

44 Ibid., 214.

45 Seremetakis 1991, 506.

alistic screaming constructs the social dimensions of any Bakhtiari's death to the extent that it carves out a topography of defilement through sound. All those who hear the ritual, even if they are not participating directly in it, are therefore implicated.[46]

Other important elements and ritualistic gestures which Bakhtiari women perform during *Gageriveh* rituals are beating their chests, pulling their hair out and scratching their arms and faces. Each level of these corporeal disorders suggests deeper and deeper dimensions of their pain as well as separation from their tribal social order.

Based on my ethnographic fieldwork as well as my long-term participation in such ceremonies, I can also confirm that, for the Bakhtiari women, pain is considered indispensable to the production and reception of truthful discourse in *Gageriveh* rituals – pain is a value that unites the biographical, historical and emotional dimensions of laments.[47] Bakhtiari women's concept of pain during *Gageriveh* rituals entangles the material and ideal, individual and collective, conceptual and performative dimensions of their deep and sad emotions for their beloveds.

Concluding remarks

Perhaps Durkheim has created a lasting influence on the anthropology of death by emphasizing that the individual grief experienced at the death of another human being is expressed collectively, in culturally prescribed ways of mourning. Grief may be a universal emotion of bereavement, as psychologists such as Bowlby have noted, but its social expression in mourning is culturally specific.[48] Therefore, Bakhtiari *Gageriveh* rituals should be understood in relation to other losses that provoke their personal and collective crises. Mourning for Bakhtiari women becomes then a social and psychological way to cope with any significant loss, for which death is the ultimate metaphor. Bakhtiari *Gageriveh* helps to draw female members of families, clans and tribes closer together and invigorates their weakened social groups. The foundation of Bakhtiari women's *Gageriveh* is *the* impression of the loss which the clan feels when one of its members dies. This very impression, however, results in bringing individuals, especially

[46] For an example, watch: Khosronejad 2004.
[47] Seremetakis 1990, 483.
[48] Bowlby 1980.

women, together, in putting them into closer social relations with one another, in associating them all with the same mental state, and, therefore, in disengaging a sensation of comfort which compensates the original loss. Because Bakhtiari women weep together, they hold onto one another and the group is not weakened, despite the blow which has befallen it. Communicating in sorrow is still communicating, and every communion of mind, in whatever form it may be made, enhances social vitality.

I believe that *Gageriveh* becomes for the Bakhtiari women an avenue for social commentary on the larger world, rather than an instrument of restriction and isolation. To hear a lament improvised is not merely to hear one person sing, but to hear an entire social ensemble vocalize.[49] Further, I believe *Gageriveh* helps those women who mourn to resolve their grief by merging their voices into a deeper lyrical persona: others have known this pain; others will feel it in the future, too. *Gageriveh*'s rhymes and meters help Bakhtiari women to organise their words and discipline their deep and sad emotions. Most of all, poetry melds their visions regarding death, bravery and heroism. *Gageriveh*, then, enables the bereaved to distance themselves from personal grief, to admit the loved one's death and to assert his immortality. It also reveals that, by means of lamentation (*Gageriveh*), Bakhtiari women can articulate their grief and locate their beloveds' deaths in larger sociopolitical and tribal contexts – and so begin to reorder and renew larger social contexts. Women, by lamenting, singing songs of loss and emphasizing in their stories the intensity of their reactions to loss, as well as through their personal involvement in mourning, simultaneously assert the weakness of their faith and the greatness of their vulnerability and attachment to others.[50]

Bakhtiari *Gageriveh* should not be read only as a personal expression that allows us to evaluate the individual women who lament. As expressions of deep attachment, Bakhtiari *Gageriveh* and songs of loss share a deep relationship with folkloric and tribal symbols. These are fundamental to understanding the meaning and sociopolitical and cultural effects of Bakhtiari tribes' discourses on death. I believe that through funeral ceremonies, as well as *Gageriveh* and its symbolic elements, Bakhtiari women represent the structure, norms, distinctive interests, or ideals of the societies that bind

---

49 Seremetakis 1990, 506.

50 Abu-Lughod 1993, 189.

them – but with more or less success and with varying degrees of consensus. At the same time, I think, the symbolic forms of funeral ceremonies are conventionally assumed to be effective in reorganizing the understandings of the Bakhtiari. It may, of course, be that only Bakhtiari women are fully aware of what is being dramatised in lamentation performances and that men are enticed into participation because they are unaware of the implications of what they are doing. The men I talked to seemed to be as much aware as women of the meaning of *Gageriveh* performances and the symbols employed in them.

Yet, there is a rich symbolic repertoire of intense emotional and affective expressions in local and traditional Bakhtiari lamentations, poetry, song and folktales. Among the Bakhtiari, verbal art, often in the form of *Gageriveh* performed during funeral rituals, is used to indirectly express strong sentiments that otherwise cannot be expressed openly or directly.

Gageriveh rituals, then, provide the bereaved with a set of shared tribal symbols – what Lévi-Strauss has called a social myth – which enables them not only to organise their experiences of death in a culturally meaningful way but also to articulate it in a socially approved manner.[51] Bakhtiari women who sing *Gageriveh* are communicating in a symbolic language and in the context of tribal performance. The goal of a structural analysis of Bakhtiari laments is therefore to learn this language, in order to understand what is being said about death. Here, one of the important points is that the men were not able to continue the traditions of bravery and manliness, but the women have kept the memory of those triumphant days alive. This is what *Gageriveh* is about: the women keep these memories in their hearts and pass them on through the generations. Thus, today we know that the Bakhtiari tribesmen were once great warriors, the likes of whom no longer exist. In the absence of written history, oral traditions are one medium through which the Bakhtiari construct their past. Songs and ceremonies associated with funeral traditions have the larger importance of recording historical events and helping to reconstruct some part of the Bakhtiaris' identity.

For the Bakhtiari, death is not a personal but a social affair, in which the family and community are present at the deathbed, wake and funeral ceremonies. These rituals repair broken ties and reaffirm the continuity and

---

[51] Lévi-Strauss 1962, 199.

solidarity of the community. Thus, death is ritualized and given great significance. Bakhtiari collective mourning helps to bring families and clans closer together and to strengthen the social group. The social function of mourning rites is not limited to the death of individuals. Indeed, mourning is a general expression of loss for a society under threat. These cultural practices produce a high level of emotion and reinforce the attachments that hold society together. They give the Bakhtiari a comforting sense of immortality, while at the same time reassembling the group that has been temporarily disrupted by the death of one of its members. Continued analysis of the contemporary funerary traditions in Bakhtiari society will create a rich structure of detailed ethnographic and anthropological evidence for anthropologists interested in nomadic life in Iran. This evidence includes information not only on the property, social status and prestige of the Bakhtiari but also on non-orthodox rituals and beliefs – and perhaps even on individuals, notably those who are being mourned.

Bibliography

Abu-Lughod, L. 1993. 'Islam and the gendered discourses of death'. *International Journal of Middle East Studies* 25, no. 2: 187–205.

Bowlby, J. 1980. *Attachment and Loss.* Vol. 3, Loss: Sadness and Depression. New York: Basic Books& Penguin Books.

Douglas, W. 1969. *Death in Murelaga: Funerary Rituals in a Spanish Basque Village*. Seattle : University of Washington Press.

Ebersole, G. 2000.'The function of ritual weeping revisited: affective expression and moral discourse'. *History of Religions* 39, no. 3: 21–46

Huntington, R., and Metcalf, P. (eds.). 1991. *Celebrations of Death: The Anthropology of Mortuary Ritual.* Cambridge: Cambridge University Press.

Hastrup, K. 1993. 'Hunger and the hardness of facts'. *Man* 28: 727–39.

Homerin, E. 1990. 'A bird ascends the night: elegy and immortality in Islam'. *Journal of the American Academy of Religion.* 58, no. 4: 541–73.

Khosronejad, P. 2013. *Les Lions en Pierre Sculptée chez les Bakhtiari: Description et significations de sculptures zoomorphes dans une société tribale du sud-ouest de l'Iran* Vol. 2, The Anthropology of Persianate Societies UK : Sean Kingston Publishing.

———. 2011. 'Lion's representations in Bakhtiari oral tradition and funerary material culture' In *The Art and Material Culture of Iranian Shi'ism: Iconography and Religious Devotion in Shi'i Islam* (ed.) Pedram Khosronejad, 193–214. UK: I. B. Tauris Publishers

———. 2006. 'The *Shahnameh* in Bakhtiari nomadic society: anthropological aspects of the hero and heroism' *Iran* XLIV, 321–26. British Institute of Persian Studies, British Academy.

Lévi-Strauss, C. 1962. *La Pensée sauvage*. Paris: Plon.

Lifton, R. 1983. The Broken Connection: On Death and the Continuity of Life. New York: Basic Books.

Rasmussen, S. 2000. 'Grief at seeing a daughter leave home: weeping and emotion in the Tuareg Techawait postmarital residence ritual'. *Journal of American Folklore* 113, no. 450, Holidays, Ritual, Festival, Celebration, and Public Display: 391–421.

Rosaldo, R. 2005. 'Grief and a headhunter's rage'. In *Death, Mourning, and Burial: A Cross-Cultural Reader* (ed.) Antonius Robben, 167–79. Oxford: Wiley-Blackwell.

Seremetakis, N. 1991. The Last Word: Women, Death, and Divination in Inner Mani. Chicago: The University of Chicago Press.

Seremetakis, N. 1990. 'The ethics of antiphony: the social construction of pain, gender, and power in the southern Peloponnese' *Ethos* 18, no. 4: 481–511.

Thurfjell, D. 2006. *Living Shi'ism: Instances of Ritualisation among Islamist Men in Contemporary Iran*. Leiden: Brill Academic Pub.

Van Gennep, A. 1960. *The Rites of Passage*. New York: Psychology Press.

Filmography

Khosronejad, P. 2004. *The Last Lions of the Bakhtiari, Bakhtiari Death Rituals* Dedicated to D. Brooks, CNRS/IMAGE, France, 25 min. https://vimeo.com/44974664

Mortezayi, S. 2006. *Children of the Prophet,* Austria, 86 min.

Healing rituals among female Turkmans of Iran

Manijeh Maghsudi

Introduction

Medical treatment and healing are two ways that attract people who suffer from pain and desperately need a remedy. Both metaphysical and medical healing occupy the domain of the experimental and the repetitive. In the beliefs and conventions of past and present societies, healing has always enjoyed a specific status. The need for remedy has formed in human beings and has driven them toward both realms.

Healing and medical treatment could be placed on a spectrum, with healing at one end and medical treatment at the other. The indigenous methods of curing a patient are termed, simply, 'healing'. They provide not an absolute remedy but a treatment aided by various physical phenomena – i.e., dramatic gestures and movements, music or the consumption of medicinal herbs – that shape several stages in the patient's recovery. These methods indicate that the process of treatment is not only finalized by metaphysical forces but rendered with the help of physical phenomena, too. However, the role played by metaphysical forces over the course of treatment – from the standpoint of those who resort to indigenous healing methods – is very significant. Throughout this article, the term 'healing' refers to the indigenous treatment method and its rituals and should not be confused with classic medical treatment. Healing seems to be related more to traditional communities, whereas medical treatment is linked to modern societies. Considering traditional communities in Iran, we find the existence of various healing methods among small scale societies such as Turkman, Kurds, Baluches and those residing in the south of Iran. Despite similarities between healing methods, in terms of their appearance, each one has certain characteristics rooted in the specific tribal milieu, as well as in their particular cultural, ethnic and geographic realities.

Healing is not a simple treatment but a ritual process that often is accompanied by certain formalities and magical ceremonies, such that the patient, the healer and the persons accompanying the patient all become inseparable constituents of the process. We should, therefore, consider the ritual and healing ceremonies as a unified whole to be explored and investigated further. Turkman indigenous treatment is reflected in various methods, the most important of which are *Ishani* and *Porkhani*. This article focuses on the ritual ceremony of *Ishani* among Turkman, exploring women healers and their personal methods. Based on ethnographic observation, this article is part of an extensive research project that has been underway in the region of Turkman Sahara of Iran for several years and is ongoing.

Presentation of Iranian Turkmans

As one of the tribes of Oghuz – one of the great tribes of Central Asia – Turkmans are known as Seljuk Oghuz because of the name of their leader, Seljuk. During the ruling era of the Samanid dynasty (819-999), in the tenth century, they were given permission to settle in the northeast area of the Iranian plateau (Moin 1993, 387). A short while after the overthrow of the Samanids and the establishment of the Ghaznavid dynasty (977–1186), some Turkman tribes received permission from Sultan Mahmud Ghaznavi (971-1030) to settle in the present lands of the Iranian Turkmans, now called the Turkman Sahara (Moin 1993, 387). Following several wars, the Iranian plateau decreased in size and some areas of it became the present countries of Afghanistan and Turkmanistan (Goli 1987, 70–71). The larger society of Turkman likewise was divided into two smaller communities: Turkmans of Iran and Turkmans of Turkmanistan (Logashva 1979, 23–24). Of course, due to the invasion and triumph of the Seljuks, a large number of Turkmans were scattered into small ethnic groups in neighbouring countries.

The actual Iranian Turkman Sahara region is located in Golestan province where in addition to Turkmans, other ethnical minorities such as Fars, Balouch, Uzbek, Kazak, Turk Azeri and Afghan immigrants yearly. Statistics regarding the population in this province cannot, therefore, serve as a reliable reflection of the Turkman population. However, according to the estimates included in Wikipedia's statistical record, the population of Turkmans reached around two million inhabitants in 1997.

Religious backgrounds

Turkmans used to live beside other tribes in Central Asia, groups such as Kalmyks, Quirqiz, Uzbeks, Tatars and Mongols. Through three large-scale immigrations, which have taken place since the tenth century, Turkmans came to the Iranian plateau from Central Asia, where Buddhist, Manavist, Animist, Totemist, Shamanist, Mazdak and Zoroastrian beliefs were common (Azami Rad 2003, 15). It is, therefore, natural that today Turkman's culture and tradition present some parts of above ideologies, or at least become familiar with them. Iranian Turkmans are all Sunnites and belong to the branch of Hanafite. Among them, especially Gooklans, the *Naghshbandieh* sufi order and related believes are quite popular and common. Also there are individual Turkmans who call themselves *Ulad* and attribute their family tree to Rashidin Caliphates (c. 632–661). They are, in turn, divided into four groups: Sheikh, Makhdum, Ata and Khujih (Maghsudi 1989, 74).

Presentation of various healing methods among Iranian Turkmans

There is no one word to define indigenous treatment among Turkmans comprehensively; they use several terms for this purpose. Depending on the nature of the treatment and the method of the healer's work, one of several terms could be applied to this practice. Each of the words, including *Ishani*, *Porkhani*, *Damar Tutan*, *Gherk Yassin*, sucking the mouth, bone-setter and *tebib* (medic), refers to a particular healing method.

Of course, for the aim of our research, the cultural origins of each of above terms should be considered and as far as the practical aspect is concerned, I believe that the term 'indigenous treatment', from a holistic view, could cover all of these activities. During my personal experiences and through the studies I conducted among Turkmans, I became more convinced of the appropriateness of applying this phrase.

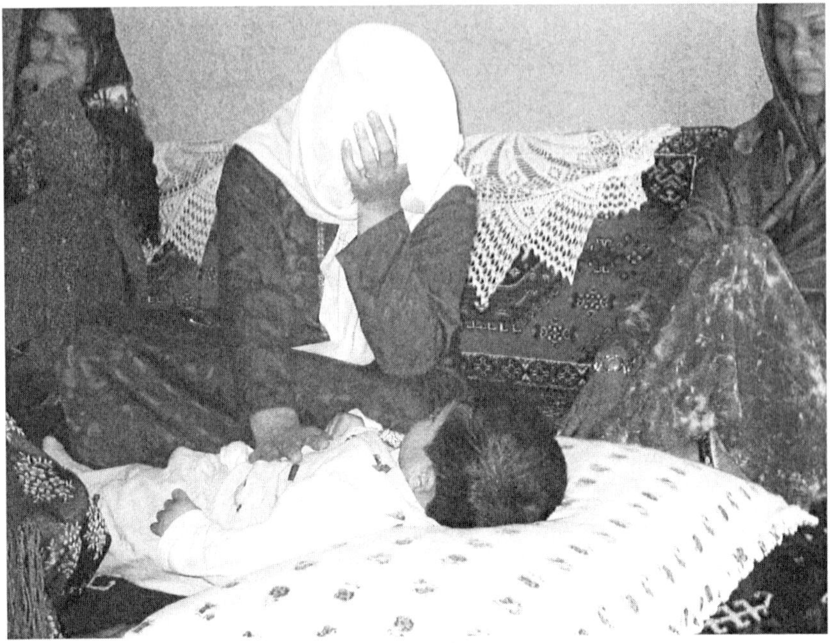

Figure 1: Hajji Ghushan village, Gunbad Kavus© Maghsudi 2010

Ishani phenomenon

If Turkman healing methods are viewed on a spectrum, one end could be said to belong to the *Porkhanis*' healing method while the other is related to the *Ishanis*'. The latter features some Islamic characteristics, too, whereas the former includes certain Shamanistic elements. *Ishani* exists among men and women alike. An important point with regard to *Ishani* treatment is its co-directionality with Islamic particulars, as well as its relationship to metaphysical forces.

Generally speaking, there are three different and distinct views toward Turkman traditional healings regarding Islamic issues. One of them is a formal view; the second one is a specific interpretation based on jurisprudents as well as to independent thinkers; and the third view is that of the public (Rajabian Tamak 2004, 30, 37–38).

According to formal Islam, these healing methods, particularly *Porkhani*, are rejected and prohibited. Here, interference with metaphysical phenomena and affairs, especially penetrating and mastering them, are

Figure 2: Hajji Ghushan village, Gunbad Kavus© Maghsudi 2010

beyond a human's capability. People are only able and allowed to seek help from God and the saints through prayer and good deeds. Or, we might remain inactive, mere observers of non-natural phenomena (such as miracles). Human beings are incapable of manipulating these phenomena or exerting their will over them. As a result, the majority of Islamic jurisprudents and independent thinkers regard the healing procedure with utmost doubt and do not give it much credence. Of course, certain local religious leaders support *Ishans* in a very conservative way. Hence, it is only in the local popular culture– and mostly among the lower classes of rural society – that the healing ritual enjoys a high status.

Generally speaking, there are two groups of *Ishans* (healer) among Iranian Turkmans. One is composed of ordinary ones, the other with exceptional aptitude. The former group consists of those who have attended theological schools and religious educations in a classical way. Afterward, through their own choice of a devotional and ascetic life, they have obtained a spiritual ranking and embarked on the profession of prayer-writing for patients. They are thus called 'prayer writers' or 'prayer writer clergymen'. This group is excluded from the scope of this investigation, which concentrates on the second group: *Ishans* who enjoy exceptional capabilities. Hereafter, in our research *Ishan* refers to the latter group.

The group of *Ishans* who are topic of our research, also could be divided into two sub-groups. The first comprises healers who have passed lengthy courses of religious studies, prayed a lot and preformed long periods of *zikr*, fasted and lived an ascetic life, but also had experienced a sudden drastic change and spiritual internal changing in their life. The second sub-group belongs to those who – like *Porkhans* – have not received religious teachings or are illiterate but nevertheless have experienced an unexpected internal transformation, without attempting to achieve this inner transformation. Members of both sub-groups gain knowledge of their new auras and spirits through psychological upheaval and bodily confusion (such as being struck by a certain sickness). Daydreaming and illusions might either follow from this situation or begin with such a process. This change of mood is interpreted by their relatives as a sign that one has been spiritually designated to render healing services and that, to this end, he or she has been endowed with special and exceptional abilities. The two groups, despite taking different routes to reaching the inner revolt, now set forth on a common path to becoming healers (Maghsudi 2009).

Initiation of young females

The initiation of young girls for becoming an *Ishan* at first begins with their daydreams. Upon seeing certain religious figures in their dreams, they discuss it also with others and finally describe it to the local sage person. One of the core interpretations of such dreams is that she should become a healer. Once one of such girls told to me:

I was told that the interpretation of my dream is the fact that I was supposed to receive a message through this dream. The message is that I should begin the healing practice, as I was designated for this purpose. I should therefore go to an experienced *Ishan* to gain necessary trainings in this respect… I therefore looked for a well experienced *Ishan* and after finding her, I told her about my dream, and she said that I should stay in her home for a few days in order to get familiar with *Ishani* life and related healing methods.

The next stage is the acceptance and approval of *Ishan*. In other words, by studying the mental and psychological states of the candidate and evaluating her claims. The healer should determine whether the candidate has exceptional abilities and if she has been designated for the task of healing, or whether she lies or is merely a sick person. If the candidate is identified as a chosen healer, she is then introduced to a local religious leader to run further related exams. If the candidate successfully passes all of these tests, she spends again sometime in the house of *Ishan* in order to undergo a course of spiritual refinement and learn the different stages of *Ishani* practice.

After the candidate has taken up residence in the house of an *Ishan*, the initiation to *Ishani* rite takes place in several ceremonial steps. The new trainee should stay one night in the shrine of Tikkiyeh Baba. Each of the Turkman healers goes to this shrine on specific nights, and *Ishans* go there on Tuesday and Thursday nights. During these two nights, a large number of middle-aged *Ishans*, young healers who have recently become healers, as well as several young girls who have experienced daydreaming, gather in this sacred place and meet to gain knowledge of each other's learnings. They likewise become acquainted with the experiences of the new and elders healers.

In this gathering, after collective ablution, women all pray; perform some *zikrs* and read the holy Quran. Also on such nights, some healers come to this place with their own patients.

Generally speaking, *Ishanis*' teachings are concentrated on one's observation of religious directives, such as conducting long prayers, five periods of daily prayer, midnight prayer, fasting and complete covering of hair and head. These trainings gradually become main part of their daily and private lives and conduct. The new students are requested to take off their colourful Turkman scarves and to use white scarves to enforce their status as a good Muslim. Instead of wearing the long golden necklaces that ordinary Turkman women use, the candidates should wear long rosaries and use them during their *zikrs*.

New arrivals also shed their Turkman clothes and don a kind of dress that likewise represents their inclination toward becoming more religious directed. They therefore set aside their traditional Turkman trousers and instead wear simpler and longer clothes. The wearing of Turkman trousers usually means that women's bare ankles can be seen, particularly because

Figure 3: Khazak women waiting for healer, Gurgan© Maghsudi&Ashtari 1978

Turkmans are not used to wearing socks. They also are encouraged to commit themselves to fasting during the months other than Ramadan.

Wearing identical clothing serves to unify young arrivals and creates the sense that they belong to a special group and should make additional attempts to reach the rank of *Ishani*. Moreover, this practice could also serve as a type of propaganda for *Ishani* ritual, contributing to its dissemination to other individuals living in the region.

Revision of one's daily conduct and behaviours constitutes part of the training that the newcomers should receive. Watching television and listening to music are totally excluded from one's daily programs. Bit by bit, they are even banned from attending matrimonial ceremonies, feasts where music is played and gatherings where men and women are not segregated. Their associations will hence be limited to their own gatherings. Zobeideh one of the new arrivals explained this issue to me by stating her own example:

Last year, upon the occasion of my daughter's marriage ceremony, the family of the groom said that they had invited an orchestra and would hold a feast in the house. I clearly told them that I would not take part in a gathering where music is played or men and women are not separated from each other, even if it was the matrimonial of my own daughter. My daughter likewise insisted to me to give permission to this program as one time happening in life, and reasoned that a matrimonial could not be held without dancing or using musical instruments and songs. However, I declined her request.

The socialization process of the new students is, therefore, accomplished in the house of an *Ishan*. The new trainees gradually become accustomed to life in seclusion and are distanced from gatherings other than their own. They will in time, be restricted to their own community. Living beside a master healer also provides the new trainee the opportunity to observe the healing ritual ceremony more closely.

Having passed a certain amount of time in the house of an *Ishan*, the candidate is prepared for the practice of healing. The duration of this practical training depends on the spiritual and physical states of the candidate. However, she is still not granted permission to lead an independent healing service. She must stay longer in the house of her master and continue her learning. When the candidate feels that she is ready to begin her job, the *Ishan* evaluates her abilities and determines whether or not she is ready. If this condition is met, she is then considered capable of becoming independent and performing the treatment of other patients alone.

A case study in a healer's house

The healing ceremony conducted by *Ishans* involves certain specific formalities. The new trainees are present for such rituals and witness the progress of procedures. Certain patients who are severely ill are taken care of in the house of *Ishans*, alongside their family members. Healers encourage the patients to follow severely their religious duties. They should pray, read the Quran, perform *zikrs*, fast and stand to midnight prayers on a regular basis. When at their homes, *Ishans* do not expect the patients to do anything. They are entertained completely and are merely advised to conduct their religious duties. All the works of the household are thus accomplished by the new trainees and also by a group of cured persons who have retained their connections to the *Ishan's* home. Principally, healers do not have any duties other than teaching the new candidates, taking care of the sick and remaining awake for the purpose of performing their religious duties. Consequently, suitable spiritual and psychological conditions are created for the patients to enjoy a long period of rest and relaxation.

Healers more or less contend that all problems afflicting a patient are due to *jinn*'s penetration into their bodies. They hence read Quran and perform certain prayers and *zikrs* in order to exorcise them from the body of the sick person. They tell their patients, 'You have been haunted by the *jinn*, and I have to drive them out of your body.' All the actions used by healers for this purpose are performed through a ritual ceremony.

A student of mine who was living in the region became my guide and accompanied me on this visit to a female healer's house. At first, we could not find her address and lost our way. In one of the poor districts, we were in a dusty alley off of the main street and, questioning the neighbours, we finally found her home. We entered her house through an arched doorway leading to the yard, which was completely open. We climbed some steps and entered a medium-sized hall. Several women were sitting around the room. Very calmly and without making any noise or paying attention to anyone or anything there, they were absorbed in a state of ecstasy and relaxation. On the right side of the hall, two other rooms and a large kitchen could be seen. This hall ended with another room, situated on the other side. Someone opened the door and led us to the other room, which was two meters long and three meters wide. Facing the room was a half-constructed wall, and it seemed that they wanted to a make a window for it in the future. This short, windowless wall faced a vast plain. When we were sitting in the room, we could see the field in front of us. We could detect some poultry moving around in total freedom and taking grains from the ground. A little further away, several cattle were grazing, and the pleasant breeze blowing from the desert had a calming effect on one's spirit. This atmosphere was indeed pleasing and gracious.

I had no idea how this meeting would be. I had come to visit a female healer, and I had only heard that she practiced healing patients through the *Ishani* method. This was my first meeting with an *Ishan*. I had no preconceived thoughts and could not imagine how this woman would appear, how she treated the sick, and what particulars the healing method employed in principle.

I sat in silence for a while, until the door opened and Zobeideh *Ishan* (healer) stepped into the room. She is a woman of around forty years old who has four children, which the last one is a newborn baby. Her mental and physical capacities influence her visitors. Her looks seem to shatter all boundaries, going beyond gender and the frames established by norms, traditions and culture. Comparing her looks with those of ordinary Turkman women, one is convinced of her special and exceptional power. This woman has completely dedicated her life to the task of curing patients and taking care of them.

When half an hour passed, the newborn was brought to her to be fed. She took the child – who was likewise big and seemed strong – in her arms, and while she was enthusiastically answering my questions, she simultaneously fed him. She seemed to have become one and the same with her profession of healing as she eagerly talked about her healing experiences. The baby also seemed to be accustomed to this method of feeding. Inattentive to the noise and chaos around him, he continued sucking milk from the breast of his mother, swaying his head around from time to time. Inattentive to my presence and that of the male guide who was with me, she unheedingly put her breast into the mouth of her baby to feed him, and at the same time lectured for us with a clear and strong voice.

After a time, a woman in non-Turkman dress came in, took the baby from her, placed him in her own arms and left the room. I became curious about this non-Turkman woman and asked about her. Healer said that this woman was one of her patients. She then gave a full profile of her sickness, as follows.

Not long ago, this non-Turkman woman was afflicted by a severe depression. She was referred to many doctors to be cured; however, no one could treat her. One day, when she was in the depth of hopelessness, one of her friends advised her to come to me. After several visits and the practicing of various healing methods for her, recovery began to take place.

Later I (author) had the opportunity to speak with this patient and asked about her feeling with respect to her presence in healer's house. She said:

> "This healer's house enjoys a strange and specific atmosphere. Whenever I come to her house, my bad mood removes and a good spirit overcomes me. I only sit in one corner and that's it. Gradually, I feel lightness in my psyche, and I don't know myself what happens here."

This woman used to come to the healer woman's house whenever she could, and she felt relaxed and remedied merely by being there. In the meantime, she felt at home in this place and that she could do anything she wanted, from taking care of the baby to washing the dishes and cleaning the house or cooking a meal.

In this way, I came to know the prevalent atmosphere of this house. Through other explanations given by the healer herself, I learned that this house was not an ordinary one but a praying place, like an abbey. It also served as a resting place for the sick and a house of hope for all the patients.

Healer's wages

It is a common practice that the healers do not receive any wages directly from patients. However, each and every person pays a certain amount of money to the healer, depending on his or her financial situation. They give the sum to her in such a way that no one notices. This is one of the main differences between a medical doctor and a healer. *Ishans* never speak about their wages to the patients directly. They usually tell them that they have dreamed that a religious figure said that a particular sum of money should be paid to them, or that they have been inspired to receive this or that amount, depending on the sickness and its intensity; that is, the wage varies according to the need. Usually, consumable items, such as sheep, chickens, oil and rice, are included in this wage, prepared, cooked and distributed to the participants in the ritual by the cured patients and the new trainees. The healer sometimes says to the patient or to her relatives that if they do not supply these things, the *jinn* will not leave the body; the illness will remain there forever and might even get worse. The healer, of course, maintains that these instructions have been given to her in a dream, and by bringing up the name of a *jinn*, she renders a frightening spiritual mood. Therefore, in their dread of the *jinn*, of the recurrence of the illness, or of its not being remedied at all, and due to their fear of the healer, they purchase the above items. However, the healer's request from them for the above arrangement does not occur only once; as long as the patient remains in her house and lives there it will be repeated from time to time. In some cases, these requests are made by the *Ishan* on behalf of a certain *jinn* or a religious personality that she has seen in her dreams, and she emphasizes that she only has the duty to convey this message to the patients and their family members. As per the healer's own claim, this request tends to increase. That is, when the trend of recovery begins to take place, the material requests increase, too. Simultaneously, the patients' fear penetrates within them more deeply and even becomes chronic. Fear that the *jinn* will not leave their bodies but will continue its presence, dread of the recurrence of illness and its getting more acute, or simply the mere fear of the healer are all factors that make the patients captives of them and cause greater dependence on the healer, both spiritually and psychologically.

In most cases, after the complete recovery of the patient from the disease the healer holds a magnificent feast in the patient's house. The expenses for these feasts are borne by the patient or by her relatives. This stage serves as the climax and final point of the treatment process.

All requested meals and consumable materials will be purchased by healer's new trainees or by some of the patients who reside in the healer's house. All the meals are distributed among the guests in the form of alms dedicated to the treatment of the patient by the healer. A portion of the alms is likewise given to the near and far neighbourhood, and to the poor living in various districts. When they ask about the reason of this alms-giving, they are told that the *Ishan*, was the cause for the patient's recovery from the illness.

Every Thursday night, this program is held in the healer's house. She is, therefore, said to have arranged an alms-giving ceremony. People from near and far come to her and ask each other about patients who have recently recovered. In this manner, the story of *Ishan*'s treatment circulates by word of mouth. This kind of association and social gathering serves as propaganda for healing profession of *Ishans*. Gatherings of those recovered from illnesses, and ceremonies in the form of lunch and dinner parties given as alms, strengthen the contentions and beliefs of the people and promote the fame and credibility of *Ishan* as a healer bestowing complete recovery on the sick. In this way, the healing phenomenon grows and develops further in the concerned region. Each of the healers spends the received money in certain ways, and none of them say directly that they use it for their own daily expenditures. Without exception, they all claim to use the money for the sake of God's satisfaction.

Concluding remarks

Over the course of this study, and throughout my close observation and interviews, my mind was constantly busy comparing this way of traditional healing system to that of the field of modern medicine. This served as a theoretical guiding tool to build a clear picture of the different aspects of healing practice. The rest of this article is thus dedicated to this comparison.

One of the first points I noticed in this respect is that female Turkman healers visit their patients as well as the patient's relatives in the same room. While they are all present in one place, they explain to the healer their personal problems, their physical, psychological and psychosomatic predicaments and dilemmas, and even discuss their family troubles in front of other people. They do not, therefore, fear the fact that others will have information about their affairs. In rare occasions, it happens that the patient asks for privacy to explain her problems, far from the crowd. She whispers into the healer's ears but is likewise aware that the others could know her situation by one look, one hint, a single word or through observation.

Personal problems are thus asserted in front of others: everyone understands what has happened, and there is no boundary or hidden secret for the patient. Feeling sympathy with others and the fact that one is not the only person who suffers from certain difficulties is, in essence, and reflected by such a mechanism.

In modern medicine, on the other hand, all dialogues are conducted behind closed doors and in a private setting between the patient and the doctor, who is regarded as the patient's intimate. With this practice, whereby the patient is alone, her problems considered private and hence kept as a secret by the doctor; likewise, this reflects the mechanism prevailing in modern medicine.

In the traditional healing method, the healer is busy with the patient. However, in modern medical practice, the doctor deals with the cause of the illness. In other words, a healer devotes all of her time to the patient: watching her, staring into her eyes, listening carefully to what she says and establishing connections with her by touching different parts of her body in order to get closer to her. In this way, a healer deals with a patient without any intermediary.

A healer's occupation with the sick person renders their activities as non-specialized, and their view in the treatment of disease is a holistic one. However, in modern medicine treatment activities are divided in several specializations, each treating a certain illness. Rendering classification is, in essence, an attribute of science and scientific methodology – and absent from the practice of traditional healers. By employing certain healing methods, such as treatment by medicinal herbs, massage, sounds and reciting prayers, the healer endeavours to remove the problems of a patient.

The patient sees a healer as a person who preserves her health, so she is considered a saviour and a link between the physical and metaphysical worlds. The healer thus becomes an intermediary between these two domains. However, a physician is seen by a patient as a person who has significant information about the treatment of a sickness, and the remedy is regarded as the physician's task. But, in the case of a healer, healing is not her duty and she is only an intermediary for the purpose of curing a patient. In effect, the relationship established between the patient and the healer promotes the spiritual aspect of the latter, and sometimes even develops toward infinity.

Bibliography

Azami Rad, G. 2003 *Nigahi Bi Hayat-i Madi va Manaviy-i Turkamanha*. Mashad: Mashad University Press.

Goli, A. 1987 *Seyri Dar Tarikh-i Siyasi-Ejtimaiy-i Turkamanha*. Tehran: Nashr-i Elm.

Logashva, B. 1979 *Trukmanhay-i Iran*. Trans. Hossein Tahvili and Cyrus Izadi. Tehran: Shabahang.

Maghsudi, M. 1989 'Family and Kinship among Iranian Turkmans'. *Ph.D. Thesis*. Paris: University of Sorbonne.

——— 2006 *'Zanan-i darmangar-i bumi dar Turkman Sahra: dar Iran va Ghafghaz' International Conference*. Armenia: Arya University.

——— 2008a 'Moghayisiyi miyani Porkhani va Ishani'. *Conference of Traditional Medicine*. Iran: Tehran.

——— 2008b *Ensanshinasiy-i khanivadih va khishavandi*. Tehran: Shirazih.

——— 2009 'Moghayisiy-i miani Porkhani va Ishani.' Conference presentation. Tehran: Iran

Moin, M. 1993 *Farhang-i Shish Jeldiy-i Moin*, vol. 6. Tehran: Farhang-i Elam.

Rajabian Tamak, S. 2004 *Rad-i Owham Bar Asasi Ghoran va Sonnat*. Mashad, Shiykalislam Ahmad Jam.

Feelings, funerals and female Muslim-Hui in southwest Shandong China

Su Min

Introduction

Chinese Muslims are portrayed by many scholars as a unified whole. The most widely cited theories for analyzing issues of Muslims and Islam in China are ethnicity or ethnic identity (e.g., Gladney 1991; Gladney 1998; Atwill 2006) – and, recently, the theory of the globalization of Islam or religious revival (e.g., Gillette 2000; Qian 2004; Ma 2006). Among these studies, several pay sufficient attention to female Muslims in China. The most influential book is on women's mosques in central China, written by Jaschok and Shui (2000). However, its discussion is much more focused on the history of Islamic mosque schools and religious education. As for studies of minority women in China, there are several articles examining concepts of women in religious teachings and historical descriptions of women's liberation (Ding 1996; Gao and Ding 1996). Presently, as far as female Muslims are concerned, great attention is paid to topics such as the control of women from religious aspects and contemporary religious movements. For example, the education of Muslim girls is considered one of the most important themes, and religion is often regarded as one of the key elements that explain Muslim girls' lack of official education (Luo 2007). Among these ethnographies and historical studies of Muslim images in China, very few thorough studies examine the daily lives and ritual practices of Muslims in contemporary China. Some scholars think of female Muslim-Hui[1] in China as marginalized in community activities, espe-

[1] In official discourse, Hui is one of the minorities in China. Han is the majority. Before the 1950s, all Hui people were regarded as Muslim, and Islam was called 'Hui jiao'

cially in funerals and other religious practices. Hence, the effect of female Muslim-Hui in rituals and at other levels must be carefully investigated.

In this chapter i explore feelings and emotions among female Muslim-Hui in rituals, specifically the representation and interpretation of women's feelings. It discusses the ways in which female feeling is materialized and constructed by social meaning within the local context. Taking the funeral as an example, along with an understanding of filial piety in Chinese culture, this article reveals multiple interactions among lamentation, food and other materialized representations of feelings during this rite.

Xinxing and Guxing: the social context

In 2006, in a small Muslim-Hui village in the southwest Shandong province, an old man named Yulai was diagnosed with terminal cancer. While Yulai was waiting to be called back by Allah, his family turned to chaos. The problem was how to arrange his funeral.

Villagers have always arranged funerals according to traditional practices. Why did tradition not work here? Yulai's family was divided into two camps. His elder son-in-law was a Muslim-Hui from the city. He adhered to Xinxing (Islam in a new style), so he argued that Yulai's funeral should be held according to Xinxing teachings. In his opinion, funerals among Muslim-Hui with the belief of Xinxing are more Islamic for a 'pure' Muslim. According to Xinxing belief, the traditional religious practices, which are Guxing (Islam in old style), have integrated too many Han Chinese practices, such as wearing white mourning clothes, kneeling and crying during the funeral. For them, these behaviours are not pure Islamic habits.

However, people in the village where Yulai lived adhered to Guxing. His wife, who wore a scarf, was from a village with the belief of Xinxing. She agreed with her son-in-law, but other members of the extended family were against them. They asked the Imam in the village to tell Yulai's youngest son that Guxing funerals also accorded with Islam.

As Malinowski (1948) noted, death is the most important crisis of life in all religions. As far as a Muslim-Hui in this village is concerned, a funeral is one of the most important rituals that can be regarded as a new symbol of ethnic identity. How to arrange a funeral is generally said to be an important

---

(Hui people's religion).

difference between these two branches of Islam. Mourning clothes and the style of kneeling are always mentioned. Therefore, for Xinxing belief, these items are important aspects of religious reform, especially for a funeral. According to Xinxing, people should not cry during the funeral, as death is an issue of predetermination. All dead people are called back from Allah; therefore, the living people should remain calm.

Who is correct? Whose idea is purely Islamic? This is not the root issue. The questions here include: why is debate over pure Islam so important? Why was the debate between Xinxing and Guxing highlighted among contemporary Chinese Muslims? More comprehensive research is needed on these issues. In this paper, funeral reform and the differences between Xinxing and Guxing will be a context for exploring the feelings of female Muslim-Hui in ritual practices.

Traditionally speaking, for Muslim women, particularly for the female relatives of the dead, crying or wailing is a primary activity in the funeral. The funeral is very often connected with feelings of lamentation, and crying is a materialized performance that demonstrates their sorrow. Women do not accompany Imams and other men who visit graves to cherish the memory of the dead. Most of them do not know how to pray and cannot read Quran – or they do not understand the meaning of Surats in Quran. As one of their main activities during a continuous funeral, crying is also a representation of their filial piety.

As an ongoing phenomenon, the so-called funeral reform among Muslim-Hui in southwest Shandong can be a starting point for us to understand how a female's feelings are materialized in ritual practices. Moreover, the social relations and regional networks stimulated during the funeral process reveal the kinship structure and social meanings of filial piety among Muslim-Hui families.

The bridge to heaven

Following the above example, the question becomes which aspects of women's practices are influenced by the ongoing religious reform and how these behaviours, as materialized expressions of their feelings or emotions, are constructed by local social meanings. In this regard, the procedures for funerals in different villages with different ideas of Islam must be elaborated.

Figure 1: A boy who attended a Guxing funeral wore a cap in accordance with the fourth generation ©Min 2007

For local Muslim-Hui, arranging a nice funeral for the dead person is considered to help the deceased get to heaven. In the religious narrative, walking on the bridge to heaven is a key test for a Muslim in the afterworld. The bridge would become wider for good Muslims but narrower for bad Muslims. Whether he is a good or bad Muslim, an Islamic funeral is necessary for a man to be called back by Allah. It is the responsibility of the living to pray for mercy from Allah, and all the mercy is for the dead. On one hand, for people attending a funeral, especially for the relatives of the deceased, prayer is a performance representing their feelings for, and connection with, the dead person; on the other hand, prayer asks the living to realize the huge power of Allah and to pray for the dead in order that he can pass the test on the bridge to the heaven. The living hope that even the 'not very good' Muslim will be punished less in the afterworld if his relatives, friends and other Muslims pray for him continuously.

Relatives of a dying Muslim-Hui person may ask the Imam in the village to recite some confessional sutras in the Quran. With his last breath, the dying one is also reminded to read Qingzhenyan (the words of purity and truth: There is no god apart from God. And Muhammad is the Messenger of God) to demonstrate and confirm that he is a Muslim who believes in Allah.

When a Muslim-Hui passes away, his family members remove his clothing. Neighbours, friends, or other relatives go to the mosque to borrow the water board prepared for funerals in the village. Propped up by two long stools, the water board is put in the principal room of the house. The dead person is laid on the board with white cotton cloth covering his body and with his face toward the west, the direction of Mecca. People also burn incense in order to keep the room pure and fresh. A white door curtain is also hung in the principal room for two or three days, until the dead person is buried.

The white door curtain separates the inside from the outside and male mourning relatives from females – both men and women belong to the mourning category. Ordinarily, five generations means a category, i.e., the *Wufu* (五服). Close relatives who are helping to prepare the funeral will inform the dead person's relatives who are of the next and preceding four generations; generally speaking, people hope for an old but not a young person's funeral. And in a common funeral, it is often related to the next and last two generations. Lineal relatives such as sons, sisters-in-law, daughters, sons-in-law, grandsons and granddaughters are required to kneel in the mourning hall. Female relatives kneel and cry beside the deceased in the principal room while male relatives gather under the mourning canopy that is temporarily built in the courtyard.

The main activities of a funeral include:

1. Send mourning message:

Neighbours and others familiar with the funeral process help to cut mourning clothes. Some of them take the bus or drive a motorcycle to other villages or cities where the dead person's relatives live. They take mourning clothes with them and send the mourning message to these relatives. Meanwhile, a money-and-gift desk called *Lidanzhuo* (礼单桌) is arranged so that people can give monetary gifts, which will be used for the funeral. Sometimes the host receives some surplus; however, after the funeral, the host will also prepare other kinds of banquets, such as the cherishing feasts on the seventh day, the fortieth day, etc. During the anniversary banquet, people may ask the Imam and others who insist on praying five times a day to recite some verses from Quran. Meanwhile, they deep-fry flour kneaded in boiling water (*Youxiang*, 油香, oiled cake) and prepare a banquet for direct relatives and Imams. There are also several young people who help dig a grave and purchase other necessities, such as camphor and borneol.

2. Pay a condolence call: People who receive mourning clothes will go to

the host's house as soon as possible. When approaching the dead person's house, they put on mourning clothes. The costumes for different generations are alike but not identical; others can discern one's relationship with the dead person from the mourning clothes. When walking toward the principal room, both women and men cry while calling the dead person's title according to their relationship, for example, 'my grandpa' or 'my uncle'. When the mourning relatives (females in the principal room and males outside) hear that someone is coming they should receive the condolence call answering with a cry. Often, women cry more loudly and for longer periods. As visitors arrive for the condolence call, females should enter the principal room but males remain outside the gate or stay in the mourning canopy. When other people who are not close relatives hear the message, such as the family's members' friends, they can pay a call, too. People who are not in the five generations but have a kindred relationship with the host family may also receive a message – they then go to the mourning house with a white cap. Sometimes the host family prepares white caps for the guests.

Family members (often the mourning son and mourning daughter) begin to cry every day in the morning, just for half an hour after the morning prayer. This is called the 'call or cry for the gate of heaven' (*Hantiantangmen*, 喊天堂门).

3. Three 'Islamic steps':

For the Muslim-Hui, the ritual of washing the deceased's corps – called *Namanyi*[2]– demonstrates cleanness and religiosity. For a deceased Muslim-Hui, it is a necessary step before the burial rite. To be clean is to be religious, which to the Muslim-Hui means that Allah loves them. Participants must have had a bath ritual; they must be clean in the religious sense. During the washing, Imams, including the one in this village and others who are invited to attend the funeral, sit in the courtyard. All people, except the helper for the bath ritual, gather in the courtyard, too. Imams stand, one after another, to give a speech. The topics are often the beliefs of Muslims, the afterworld and the power of Allah. Sometimes the goal is to demonstrate the existence of Allah so that people who are in doubt or who do not obey Allah's requirements, such as five prayers every day, can learn more about the belief.

The procedure is for the dead Muslim-Hui to wear *Kefan* (white clothes, 穿克番). Shiny clothes are not permitted. Moreover, nothing else can be buried with the deceased. A white cap is also needed for the dead, for both men and women. However, recently in the Guxing village, the female dead have sometimes been dressed with a scarf. It is said that they have learned from the Xinxing people. Camphor and borneol are sprinkled on the white clothes to deter insects. People also put *Qiqiaomi* (七窍米, rice in the seven holes) in the deceased's mouth, nose, ears and so on.

The deceased is then put in a large phylactery and carried to the courtyard. The next step is the most important in Islamic terms: the stand rite, that is, *Janaza* (者那则 in Chinese). Local people say that the deceased would not know that he or she were dead until Imams and other Muslims held the stand rite for them. Furthermore, the more Muslims who attend this ritual,

2 *Manyi* means the dead person's body. It has the same pronunciation as the Chinese word '满意', which means satisfaction

the more love is given by Allah. It may show that the deceased is a good Muslim-Hui who received love and esteem during his life. More importantly, local people consider it to be a ritual that mitigates their debts in life and diminishes punishment from Allah.

4. Deliver the burning incense and deliver the lection (Quran):

After the stand rite, Imams, *Hai'erpai*[3] and *Xianglao* (乡佬, several villagers in charge of the mosque) will take the burning incense and deliver it in turn.

Then the lection begins. Relatives of the dead person, such as the mourning son (*Xiaozi*[4], 孝女) and mourning daughter (*Xiaonv*, 孝子), daughter-in-law, son-in-law, grandsons and granddaughters are included; it takes several rounds. Imams and Xianglao stand in a circle. Money enveloped in white paper is put on the table. All of those who will deliver Quran must provide enveloped money. These relatives then take up the Quran, which also is packed in white paper. They first say 'Dadan'[5] and then deliver the Quran to the first Imam or Xianglao, who may recite a very short lection, perhaps just one sentence, and deliver it back to the person. The person then says Dadan and delivers it to the next Imam or Xianglao. This continues until the last person finishes the round. It is said that delivering Quran means that all of the Imams and Xianglao attending the ritual recite the whole book. Reciting Quran is very good for the dead person; it is seen as helping to reduce his debt from life. All return from Allah will be for the dead person ... However, for Xinxing people, it is called 'using money to buy lection'.

5. Go to the grave:

The last step is only for men. The deceased in the phylactery is carried to the grave. Imams and Hai'erpai with Xianglao take charge of the burial. Sometimes, a canopy with lection (a white cloth with one or several surats written in Arabic) can be used. It is said that not all Muslim-Hui people can use it, only those who pray and fast during their lifetimes and can read verses in Quran can have the honour of this treatment. The lection canopy reveals not only that the dead person was a devoted Muslim who knew how

---

3 They are called *manla* in northwest China. Sometimes it is translated as *mulla*; however, the word has more local meanings with its Chinese pronunciation.

4 XIaozi: xiao means filial piety; zi means son; nv means daughter.

5 It is said to be a Persian word that means agreement.

to pray and read Arabic lection but also the hope that gladness from Allah may help to reduce his debts.

Figure 2: Praying after the burial in Guxing village © Min 2003

After burying the dead, Imams, Xianglao and male relatives of the deceased return home. Imams and Xianglao recite chapters of Quran. This is called *Yuanjing*, which means making the lection satisfactory. All people there pray for the deceased person.

Religious reflection: Xinxing and its funeral

Reciting Quran to confess before death is not a step in the new-style funeral. Some hold that the Muslim-Hui should pray every day and confess every day. Therefore, it is not necessary for them to confess just before death. The Guxing notion that final confessions may save a bad person's spirit – and that the deceased can, therefore, gain some forgiveness from Allah – is regarded as having no effect in Xinxing funerals.

Although people who practice Xinxing send mourning messages and pay a condolence 'call', crying, especially keening, is not permitted. Sometimes relatives from Guxing villages may pay a voiced condolence call, which is permitted so that people may retain a good relationship with and host a harmonious funeral for the dead person. The key requirement is not to cry. For Imams and other people in Xinxing villages, these rules are considered to be from the Prophet's instructions. However, according to some Guxing Imams' interpretations, crying in the funeral also follows the Prophet's instructions – they choose instructions from different chapters.

Mourning clothes are not used in the new-style funeral. All men use white caps, and the women wear scarves. For Xinxing people, wearing mourning clothes – a custom they consider to be learned from the Chinese Han – mimics a Han funeral. However, kneeling and mourning clothes are regarded as representations of filial piety. Therefore, some people of Guxing argue that a Xinxing funeral cannot sufficiently demonstrate filial piety. And in some new-style funerals, people say that it is not good for a filial son and daughter not to cry, as they feel so bereft.

Delivering the burning incense and delivering the lection (Quran) are not among the procedures of a new-style funeral. Xinxing reinterprets these kinds of activities, arguing that delivering Quran at the funeral has no Islamic significance. Qiqiaomi is no longer used in Xinxing funerals, either. Lack of Islamic origins is an important explanation for people with Xinxing beliefs. However, Imams in Guxing villages also try to validate their behaviours according to Quran and Hadith.

Funeral without the end: Guoshi and the continuous life rite

For both the Xinxing and the Guxing, funerals last for three days at most. However, burial is a temporary end of life rite; mourning is a lasting ritual process. Taking a parent's funeral as an example, the son, daughter-in-law, daughter and son-in-law traditionally have the responsibility to perform rituals for the deceased. Family members will hold several ceremonies for the dead person, including those held on the seventh day, the fortieth day, the one-hundredth day, the first anniversary, the third anniversary, the tenth and the thirtieth. These commemorative activities are called Guoshi (过事 doing rituals).

Additionally, many Muslim-Hui also ask Imams to recite chapters from Quran for their parents on their birthdays, during Ramadan or at other important family affairs, such as a grandson's wedding, a granddaughter's entering college or university and so on. Sometimes, they just ask the Imams to recite lections in the mosque. Other times, they may go to the grave with Imam. This is called *Zoufen* (走坟 go to the grave). However, Zoufen is a formal practice that is only for men. Females can go to the grave themselves; often, they go there to have a look and cry for a moment until neighbours nearby come to help them up. Females never go to the grave with Imams. When they have the intention to Zoufen for their parents, they can give some money (twenty Yuan RMB, fifty Yuan, one hundred Yuan, etc.) to their brothers, who can go with the Imam for a formal Zoufen. On those occasions, the brothers will tell the Imam that the Zoufen is of his sisters' intention. The money called Jingli (gift for reciting verses) will be given to the Imam.

Figure 3: Before the ritual banquet on the third anniversary, some female family members went to the tomb © Min 2006

When a formal ritual, such as an anniversary, is approaching, the daughter-in-law plays a key role in preparing food and arranging relatives for the ritual banquet. Sons and daughters must purchase goats, preferably white horned goats. More than ten years ago, daughters would take a gift called Youmianli (油面礼 gift of oil and flour) to fry Youxiang. Youxiang is a necessary food on important occasions, especially during rituals for the deceased. Youxiang must not be wasted or given to animals. It is also the return gift to daughters and other relatives who attend the anniversary ceremony. All the cooks who fry Youxiang are females – they are the experts in the village. Some of them learned this task when they were about twenty years old.

Females and the materialized feelings in funerals

Funerals are important occasions for examining women's feelings and materialized representations. First, local people regard funerals as revealing important differences between Guxing and Xinxing. Second, this is the only life rite that gathers all relevant people together at one time. Meanwhile, it focuses on one of the important feelings: lamentation. During the continuous funeral practice and other rituals for the deceased, women – otherwise outsiders or potential outsiders – act as insiders again. Looking at how these communal life rites are organized and arranged, I focus on how women practice their lamentation and how female relatives interpret their representations of lamentation, which is often considered to be related to their filial piety.

Debates

The difference between Xinxing and Guxing is analyzed in terms of globalization and localization theory, especially in the discourse of religious revival. Among these, customs are seen as the key element in examining historical memory and contemporary practices. Because Islam has been constructed as a world religion in modern China, certain localized customs are seen as pivotal characteristics to be excluded and purified during the reconfirmation of Muslim identity. Among these, the funeral is one of the most important.

During the long period of communication with Han Chinese traditional culture, the culture of the Muslim-Hui in China has been multiplex and regional, especially in aspects of dress and funeral structure. For some Muslim-Hui, what is the most important element that was learned from Han popular religion or Han culture in the funeral is one of the most important questions. For many people, it is rooted in the idea of filial piety according to the Confucian tradition (filial piety is also an important teaching in the Quran). The concepts of a mourning period, wearing white mourning clothes and kneeling are regarded as those learned from the Han funeral. From the viewpoint of Xinxing, this kind of funeral is not Islamic, or not pure Islamic. However, the Guxing will choose filial piety within Islamic tradition to interpret their behaviour. In particular, many women say that we should cry during the funeral and show our feelings (especially lamentation):

'When a person dies, it is different from the death of an animal. We can bury a dog or cock with silence. How can we bury a person without any feelings?!'

Crying is regarded as an important representation through which sentiment is delivered. But people who believe in Xinxing insist that filial piety during the person's lifetime should be emphasized more: 'We should support parents when they are living. Crying at the funeral is no use for the dead one.' On the other hand, Xinxing people state that many women, such as the daughter or daughter-in-law, cry while grumbling or rebuking others. Sometimes, grumbling has to do with conflict among wives of brothers. However, the Guxing people may argue that people should be filial both during their parents' lives and at the funeral. For them, preparing rituals in order that the dead person can be less punished by Allah is also considered an expression of filial piety.

Foods with feelings: women and men

As shown above, women, particularly the daughters of the deceased, can go to the grave alone and cry for awhile without Imams present. Additionally, although sons can go with Imams who recite verses of Quran, they cannot cry there and then. During of anniversaries, for example, men (mainly the son, son-in-law and grandson) go with Imams to the grave, while women (such as daughters, daughters-in-law and granddaughters) cry loudly in the house. This is the only chance for them to cry before the ritual banquet at the community level.

Remembering is seen as an important representation of feelings for, or connection with, one's deceased parents. Remembering refers to other practical activities, such as performing rituals for them, going to the grave or giving money to the Imams while asking them to recite lections of Quran for the deceased. Among these rituals and ceremonial activities, some foods are regarded as special provisions prepared or provided by direct female relatives (especially the daughters), such as fried Youxiang, Laoshaobing (老烧饼[6]), Shaobing (baked sesame seed cake) and goat, etc. Or, people discuss daughters' contributions to the ritual as showing the importance of the ceremony:

"The most important rituals to remember the deceased are the seventh day, the first anniversary and the third anniversary. The tenth anniversary is also necessary. The host must buy or feed goats that will be slaughtered by an Imam. About the seventh day, the fortieth day and the one-hundredth day, there is no necessary responsibility for daughters to feed goats. However, in terms of the first anniversary and the third anniversary, daughters must buy or feed goats. Other relatives may take oil (mainly cotton oil) and flour. Daughters should also take cotton oil and flour. That is Youmianli."

According to local people's interpretation, all of these foods and rituals may play a role of exchange for Allah's mercy and reward (Huici, 回赐). Guoshi is still actively practised in the very important sense, particularly for people and families in Guxing villages. Whether one will receive mercy and reward from Allah depends on the intention of the rituals' hosts. For example, one of my informants said, 'if I intend to hold the ritual and slaughter goats for my parents, then the reward from Allah will go back to them.'

Youxiang and Laoshaobing

Youxiang, a very important ritual food, is fried on many occasions. When a family member enters college, a family pays off debts, or a little boy survives an accident, the family hosts may fry Youxiang. This act has the common name 'Zuozhigan (做知感)' – that is, doing a family-level ritual to fry Youxiang and distribute it in their community. When the first pot of Youxiang is fried, the hosts should go themselves, or ask others to go, to the mosque to send Youxiang to the Imam. Then, family members and direct relatives who are invited to attend the ritual begin to eat Youxiang. Meanwhile, the hosts and others begin distributing Youxiang in the com-

6 In general, Lao (老) means old. However, in the context of southwest Shandong, people also call death Lao (老).

munity. Although there are many occasions on which Youxiang is made, its essential importance still lies in funerals and Guoshi.

It has been mentioned that Youmianli was more popular ten or more years ago. As we see in this word, 'you' means oil and 'mian' refers to the most popular cooking material in north China: flour. Moreover, the third part, 'li' emphasizes the social meaning of the gift in traditional Chinese culture. 'At the beginning,[7] it was popular to take four Jin (equivalent of two kilograms) of flour and one Jin (half kilogram) of oil', a seventy-six-year-old man told me, 'Later on, it became preferable to take six Jin flour and one Jin oil. Then, presenting ten Jin flour and one Jin oil became popular.'

Nowadays, relatives and daughters may not take cotton oil and flour, but they pay money according to their connection to and relationship with the host or the deceased. The host can refuse non-direct relatives' monetary gifts while insisting on holding the ritual banquet.

Not only does Youxiang distinguish the Hui from the Han, it also is a special food for the Muslim-Hui community. It is not commonly eaten in daily life and cannot be sold in the market.[8] People often compare funerals or commemoration activities in terms of Youxiang. For example, how much flour does the host family use to fry Youxiang? One of my informants who adheres to Guxing attended a remembrance activity in the city. For her, the most important aspect worthy of mention is that it cost the host family a thousand Jin (500 kg) flour to fry Youxiang. This suggests that, on the one hand, the host family did hold a generous ritual for the deceased; on the other hand, the deceased can get great reward from Allah on the basis of the family's benefaction. In recent years, Youxiang has been increasingly impacted by the reform process as commemoration activities, such as Guoshi, have reduced in Xinxing villages. In a funeral in a Guxing village in 2007, Imam Sha, acting as the representative of the Hui community in religious affairs, appealed to villages to retrench frying Youxiang in order to save money and energy for the host family. It is consistent with the official policy on a simple funeral. Yet village people respond differently. Some people thought it to be a good idea; others regarded this as learning from Xinxing. Furthermore, as a local person named Su Chun said, 'If we don't

---

7 It means 'the beginning' in his times.

8 This is not true in every region. One can purchase Youxiang in Yunnan, Shenzhen and other places.

Figure 4: Frying Youxiang in the kitchen © Min 2003

fry Youxiang, we would be like Han people. If we are not permitted to fry Youxiang, it would be better not to be titled as Hui people!'

Therefore, Youxiang is very symbolic in this region. It is involved with traditional rituals and local rules, connecting history with current practice. Meanwhile, as far as women are concerned, married daughters act as both outsiders and insiders. They take Youmianli just like other relatives, whereas their responsibility is seen as an important function in describing ritual practice and the significance of remembering activities.

Laoshaobing has similar meanings as Youxiang before, but it gives more prominence to daughters' effect. As vice Imam Sha Deming said:

"We were previously not wealthy. At that time, the deceased's daughters took the responsibility to buy Laoshaobing as *Niyah* (乜贴)[9] to hand out among relatives who attended the funeral. It was the food to serve relatives. Nowadays, we are not poor and have no lack of food and drinking. In recent years, it has not been so popular to provide Laoshaobing. We serve meals for guests."

On the social meanings of Laoshaobing, vice Imam Sha continued to explain:

"Laoshaobing is for people to pray for condonable from Allah. However, it is not so reverent if people treat it as good for children to eat Laoshaobing. For example, some people said enfant would be longevous. It is not devotional."

The Niyah goat

Frying Youxiang is also called delivering Niyah, a type of donation giving mercy back to the one who is in the intention of the donors. Before the frying activities, all participants should have a ritual bath in the Islamic way. In other words, in addition to the cooks, the young men helpers who stir the flour with hot water should be religiously clean, too. People label the goat slaughtered for the ritual banquet the Niyah goat (乜贴羊) It shows people's intention to pray for mercy from Allah, wishing that all the mercy would go to the deceased.

---

[9] *Niyah* (also called *niyah* [Arabic: 乜贴]) is the Islamic concept of the intent one evokes in his heart to perform an act of worship for the sake of Allah. In Chinese Muslim society, Niyah has a similar meaning to *Sadaqah*, charity or almsgiving.

The goat is the most important animal among Muslim-Hui in southwest Shandong. They buy and sell goats at market, feed goats in the county and slaughter goats in many kinds of rituals. Furthermore, the images of Muslim-Hui are fabricated more with their peddler life in relation to the centrality of goats in their lives. However, for Muslim-Hui themselves, goats have many social and symbolic meanings in their daily lives.

There are three types of occasions on which goats are slaughtered with specific symbolic meanings. One is the annual ritual Eid al-Qurban (Corban Festival, 古尔邦节), seventy days after Ramadan. Another is for bereavement, such as funerals and the lasting remembrance activities described above Still another is for happy occasions, such as a wedding, and special rituals of exchanging goats for a particular person (such as a small boy).

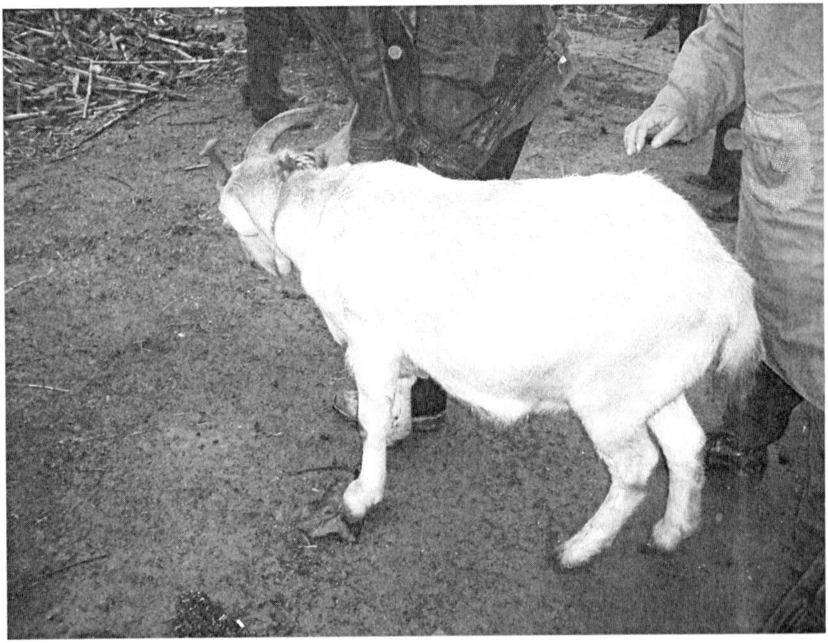

Figure 5: Niyah goat for the third anniversary © Min 2006

It has been mentioned that the Niyah goat is related to funerals and other commemoration rituals. There are some standards for local people buying goats: it must be a goat (not a sheep), be green or white, and have horns.

When discussing the Niyah goat, a seventy-five-year-old Hui woman first interpreted it as a way to show filial piety: 'Parents bring children up very hard' she said, 'According to the classical lection, sons and daughters should hold the intention to exchange Niyah goats for their deceased parents.' A middle-aged man spoke more about the symbolic meanings of the Niyah goat:

"People pay more attention in choosing goats that will be used in funeral ceremonies. Niyah goats should have horns. Horned goats can help the deceased in the afterlife go across the immortal bridge to heaven. The immortal bridge is very narrow as ox hair. While being well mounted with goats, they would be able to pass the bridge in a flash. Goats exchanged in the Corban Festival are seen as taking the important function of helping the deceased get across the bridge. Niyah goat may have the same meaning. That is why we pick horned goats. Allah is so merciful that almost all of the people could be excused in the future."

For him, Niyah goats which are regarded as related more to funerals and related rituals have something to do with the belief in an afterlife and imagination of heaven. Here he mentioned the ritual goat after Ramadan. In his narrative, people can exchange goats with their own intention when alive. However, not everyone has the opportunity to plan to slaughter goats for himself before his death. It thereafter demonstrates that Niyah goats for deceased Muslim-Hui are still necessary and considerable:

"Not everyone is qualified to slaughter goats for exchange. For example, they should be out of debt and have enough savings that they can use extra money to plan the slaughtering ritual. Hence, sometimes we see it as a festival for wealthy people."

Consequently, 'There are more old Muslim-Hui loving to slaughter goats in this ritual, particularly the retired men.' He also gave me another example to show the filial piety contained in these behaviours:

"My cousin once promised to slaughter a goat in this festival. However, on his intention, the goat was exchanged for himself, but not for my uncle, his father. I am very angry with that. He promised to exchange a goat for himself, then the benefit rewarded by Allah would be back to him. At the same time, my uncle was not wealthy and not able to slaughter a goat for himself. However, the reward in the basis of slaughtering goats is very rich and generous. When getting across the bridge to heaven, people can hold the horns and pass it in a flash. Some people slaughter goats every year. Others can also promise to slaughter goats for the deceased."

Afterward, this man commented that Guoshi is very important and should be performed seriously. For him, it is wrong for many families to attempt to save trouble. 'Some people with Guxing belief do ritual like that, too. Many of them simply leave a goat to the mosque and then finish the commemoration activity', he said, 'They don't understand the significance of Guoshi. The goat should be used to serve the guests so that they gather together to remember the deceased.'

All of these foods – Youxiang, Laoshaobing and goat – are seen as carrying filial piety so far as their ritual functions are concerned. More details are involved with filial piety among these remembrance activities which are regarded as presenting potential feelings of local Muslim-Hui, such as sorrow and lamentation. Meanwhile, it leaves female Muslim-Hui in a position to act as both outsiders and insiders in rituals, so that they are more discussed as the very parts to show the significance of rituals.

Concluding remarks

Based on in-depth interviews and participant observation, I attempted to expand on a local vision of feelings, funerals and females among Muslim-Hui in southwest Shandong province, China. In particular, my research shows how women's feelings like lamentation are constructed and materialized in funerals and remembrance activities. According to their descriptions and the interpretations of local Muslim-Hui, Youxiang, Laoshaobing and goat bear the weight of filial piety which demonstrates the sorrow and lamentation surrounding their parents' deaths. Furthermore, married daughters who act as both outsiders and insiders are discussed as the necessary and pivotal actors in revealing the significance of these rituals as they are the major protagonists in preparing those important ritual foods and in crying. Female Muslim-Hui are put in a special position to feel sorrow and express filial piety after their parents' deaths. Therefore, although female Muslim-Hui, particularly daughters of the deceased, are not in the list of pedigrees and while they do not attend the burial ritual, they occupy an important ritual position which is symbolically established in cosmological explanation.

To go further, as we see that religious activities like Guoshi are performed more actively in Guxing families, women's feelings or emotions, discussed above seem to be not as evident in the circumstances of Xinxing. Is the ritual importance of female Muslims switched or decreasing in funerals and other memorializing performances? It certainly has something to do not only with women. Because Guoshi and other memorializing rituals are not practised in Xinxing villages as before, the functions of both men and women may change gradually. As a result, the aspects in which we can examine the emotions that they express in Muslim society needs further exploration

In sum, as shown in the behaviours described above and local people's narratives, we can conclude that it is easy to analyze recent phenomena in terms of globalization theory and religious revival, but it is difficult to understand many activities of local people who practise Islam in their own ways – particularly the Muslim-Hui who insist on their 'traditional' practices. The globalization theory interprets the 'revival' of Islam in China as solely an outside influence, ignoring the local power dynamics and ritual practices. In this paper, with the theme of female Muslim-Hui and their materialized feelings, we find that it is instructive to approach 'religious revival' on the basis of detailed ethnography understanding people's choices within a more complex social context.

In the end, methodologically speaking, as a local female Muslim-Hui I took part in several funerals including those for my direct relatives. However, I never attended the final stage of a funeral: the burial. It is certainly because of my female membership in the community. In addition, when I interviewed people in Xinxing villages, I occasionally was asked to put on my scarf. Some of them assumed that I was Guxing because my native village accorded with the Guxing practice and they tried to persuade me to wear my scarf in daily life. Although we can see that some women in Guxing villages wear scarves, it has not been common until recently. On many occasions during my fieldwork, when I came back from a Xinxing village, I took off my scarf. One decision is personal choice, while another reason is more community constructed.

Bibliography

Atwill, G. D. 2006. *The Chinese Sultanate: Islam, Ethnicity, and the Panthay Rebellion in Southwest China, 1856–1873*. Redwood City, CA: Stanford University Press.

Ding, H. 丁宏. 1996. 'Examining views on women in Islam through Holy Quran' 从 古兰经 看伊斯兰教的妇女观. In *Studies on Issues of Minority Women in China* (eds.) Bai Wei 白薇, Wang Qingren 王庆仁 and Zheng Yuqin 郑玉琴, 1–17. Beijing: Central University of Nationalities Press.

Gao Z. 高占福 and H. Ding 丁宏. 1996. 'On the social status of female Muslim Hui'. In *Studies on Issues of Minority Women in China* 中国少数民族妇女问题研究 (eds.) Bai Wei 白薇, Wang Qingren 王庆仁 and Zheng Yuqin 郑玉琴, 31–47. Beijing: Central University of Nationalities Press.

Gillette, B. M. 2000. *Between Mecca and Beijing: Modernization and Consumption Among Urban Chinese Muslims*. Redwood City, CA: Stanford University Press.

Gladney, D. C. 1991. *Muslim Chinese: Ethnic Nationalism in the People's Republic*. Cambridge: Harvard University Press, Council on East Asian Studies.

———. 1998. *Ethnic Identity in China: The Making of a Muslim Minority. Case Studies in Social Anthropology* (eds.) George and Louise Spindler. New York: Wadsworth.

Jaschok, M. and J. Shui, 2000. *The History of Women's Mosques in Chinese Islam: A Mosque of Their Own*. Richmond, Surrey: Curzon.

Luo, G. 骆桂花. 2007. 'Interpretation of cultural symbols: social investigation on educational culture of female Muslim-Hui in Gansu, Qinghai and Ningxia' 文化符号. 的继承与解读–青宁回族女性教育文化的社会考察 *Qinghai Ethnic Studies* 青海民族研究 18, no. 3: 19–24.

Ma, 马福德 2006. *The Pioneer of Modern Islamic Revival: On Wahab and the Thoughts* 近代伊斯兰复兴运动的先驱——瓦哈卜及其思想研究. Beijing: Chinese Social Science Press 北京:中国社会科学出版社.

Malinowski, B. 1948. *Magic, Science and Religion, and Other Essays*. New York: Doubleday.

Qian, X. 钱雪梅. 2004. 'On the revival of Islam' 对伊斯兰复兴的 – 种认识. *Studies of International Politics* 国际政治研究 1: 99–108.

Methodological implications of the researcher's gender and religion: reflections on fieldwork with Sufi women in Istanbul

Anna Neubauer

Introduction

Feminist and other reflexive writers have demonstrated that the construction of knowledge always depends on the various personal characteristics of the researcher. While in the field, the anthropologist is never only an anthropologist but also a person of a particular gender, age, class, ethnic identity, educational background, religion and sexual orientation (Bell, Caplan and Karim 1993). In this chapter, I will elaborate on the implications of two of these characteristics: gender and religion.

The fact that all knowledge is gendered has been clear to most social scientists for some time, especially due to the work of feminist anthropologists (Abu-Lughod 1988; Haraway 1988). While feminists have become increasingly aware that the researcher's gender combines with numerous other personal characteristics in shaping the fieldwork experience, they often forget to mention belief among these characteristics.[1] My own experience reveals that religion is indeed a very important factor, especially when working with religious communities on topics related to religious practice.

Leaving aside the larger issues of representation that are beyond the scope of this article, I will focus on what happens during fieldwork. As Warren and Hackney stated: 'Gender shapes the interactions in our setting; it shapes entrée, trust, research roles, and relationships – the entire epistemological field through which we, as fieldworkers, identify our method-

[1] Caplan cites age, sexuality, ethnicity and class (1993, 19). Warren and Hackney mention age, class, ethnicity, or sexual identity (2000, ix).

ological experiences' (Warren and Hackney 2000, 3). The same can be said of religion.

To illustrate my reflections, I draw on experiences from several months of fieldwork among Sufi circles in Istanbul between 2005 and 2007. Although my research centres on one group of the Rifai tradition, I also visited other communities regularly. The group with which I spent the most time consists of disciples of Cemalnur Sargut, a female Sufi master. Her circle of close disciples comes mainly from the upper or upper-middle class, and most of them are highly qualified. The majority of the members are women, but there are also some men participating. It is interesting to note that this group does not observe any spatial gender segregation, except during prayer and other rare religious ceremonies. Women do not cover their heads, and members of the two sexes interact freely. Some of their activities, like Quran courses, take place in an informal manner in private homes, while others are lead in a more public fashion, under the umbrella of a women's cultural association.

As for the other groups, all of them have male sheikhs as spiritual guides and draw their followings from various classes. I have visited several Qadiri groups, another Rifai group, the famous Jarrahi-Khalvati lodge and a Mevlevi group. I have not been successful in finding access to any Naqshbandi groups, which have the reputation of being more closed to outsiders.

Shared characteristics: 'open sesame'?

The question I want to address in the first part of this chapter is: does sharing personal characteristics with the people one studies make research easier or more difficult? At first glance, it seems that access can be impossible, or at least more difficult, for people not sharing certain characteristics.

a. Gender

Catharina Raudvere noticed that there is always a relation between the conception of gender in the studied society and the researcher's access to data (Raudvere 2002). The extent to which gender plays a role, and how it does so, depends on how the studied community conceives gender differences. The more marked the differences between the sexes in the observed society, the more significant the researcher's gender becomes. As Muslim religious groups observe more or less strict gender segregation, these are settings in which gender promises to be an essential factor in shaping access to the field. Thus, it seems quite obvious that access to women should be easier for a person of the same sex.

Reading accounts of female researchers studying women and rituals in Muslim countries, a recurrent idea is that men simply cannot do this kind of research because they do not have access to women. This is certainly true for many Muslim communities that apply gender segregation strictly, like the one with which Raudvere worked in Istanbul (Raudvere 2002), or communities in Iran, like those studied by Mary Hegland and Sabine Kalinock (Hegland 2003; Kalinock 2004). For most of the groups I have met in Istanbul, however, the situation seems to be different.

For example, I am not certain that this idea would hold true for Raik Baba's group. Baba is a Rifai sheikh whose disciples meet once or twice a week for a *zikr* ritual. During the *zikr*, men and women are together in the same room, without a clear separation between them. It would, therefore, be very easy for a man to observe a woman's behaviour during rituals. In fact, the sheikh gives special attention to the women's active participation in the ritual – for example, asking certain women known for their beautiful voices to sing in front of the others. It would be even easier for a man to study the disciples of Cemalnur Sargut. A male researcher could be present and participate in most of their activities freely, as these are mixed instances, anyway. I am quite sure that a male researcher could conduct personal interviews with the women without major difficulties in these two groups.

I think we should be careful with this kind of claim – that fieldwork among women could never have been done by a male anthropologist – as it carries the danger of feeding what James Gregory called 'the myth of the male ethnographer and the woman's world' (Gregory 1984). Gregory argues that the traditionally accepted view regarding the inaccessibility of a woman's world to male ethnographers is largely a rationalization that justifies male anthropologists' lack of interest in women and the androcentric view they adopt in their research. He claims that women encounter the same difficulties when trying to gain access to the male world, but that they try harder then their male counterparts because the man's world is seen as too important to be simply omitted from research. Of course, as I have stated, this might vary from one society to another; Gregory himself identifies societies that practice veiling and the seclusion of women as extreme cases in which it might be nearly impossible for male researchers to obtain information about women. However, my own experience in Istanbul shows that, even in Muslim communities, this is not always the case.

b. Religion

Sharing the same religion also seems to facilitate access, as being a Muslim makes establishing rapport with Muslim communities much easier. Habiba Fathi, a French researcher of Algerian origin, remembers that her relationship with the people she studied in Central Asia became much easier when she stopped presenting herself as a French researcher and instead emphasized her Algerian and Muslim origins (Fathi 2004). Other researchers report the difficulties they faced because they were non-Muslim. Raudvere states that it took a while for statements such as 'only a Muslim can fully understand' to become progressively rarer. In the conclusion to her book, Pnina Werbner reflects at length on the difficulties she had and the conflicts that arose during her fieldwork with Sufis in Pakistan and England, because of her Jewish origins. In the lodge where she was staying, rumours started to spread that she was a Jewish spy (Werbner 2003, 296); she was also refused access to the meeting room of a British branch of the group, the reason being that she was considered an 'infidel'(Werbner 2003, 300).

During my research, I was never refused access because I am not Muslim – at least not admittedly. It is indeed plausible that my attempts to establish contact with Naqshbandi groups failed for this reason, although it was never openly stated. For the other groups, I was always surprised that people would do their best to include me in their activities, encouraging me to have the best position among them, despite the fact that they knew that I am a Christian. Thus, it is possible to be accepted as a non-Muslim, and the readiness of at least some Muslim groups to accept a Christian raises unexpected and interesting questions, especially in the field of rituals.

Actually, the question was not, as I first expected, whether it was acceptable for them that I, a non-Muslim, take part in their rituals, but whether it was acceptable for me. Everyone knows that, contrary to the pleasant phrase 'participant observation', it is virtually impossible to observe and participate at the same time. The best examples to illustrate this point are my visits to a Qadiri lodge. I have been there on five different occasions, on evenings when members of the group would gather for a *zikr* ritual. In this lodge, men and women perform rituals under the guidance of a male sheikh in a large room, separated into two halves by a wooden latticework. After joining the women's half, I had to decide if I was going to sit among the women and participate (with almost no opportunity to take notes) or, alternatively, stay at the back of the room and observe. The two first times, I accepted their invitation to participate and sat with the women in the front row, right behind the latticework. This was actually not a good position because it was difficult to see through the latticework, so I could not observe the men who were in front of me, nor the women who were behind me. It was only on the third occasion, when I felt I should gather more specific notes about the ritual, that I insisted on sitting at the back, which I did for the last three ceremonies I witnessed.

I am not sure how much one [a non-Muslim?] can learn from participating, as one cannot draw on one's own experience to claim an understanding of these women's inner experiences, not sharing fundamental theological conceptions. The reason I participated was that it allowed me to not stress my identity as a researcher too much in the beginning, although I had presented myself as such upon my arrival. I confusedly felt that sitting at the back and observing would put too great a distance between us. The strategy that I developed and applied to other groups, which worked quite well, was to minimize note-taking on the first two visits. Later, when the members knew me better, I would start moving around with my notepad.

While discussing the impact of religious difference on fieldwork, we often speak in terms of Muslims and non-Muslims. Actually, the religious border between insider and outsider is not always situated where one would expect it. I suspect that this religious border might be even more significant when separating believers (in a religion of the book) from non-believers. This idea was confirmed by a colleague of mine who also worked on religious issues in Turkey. He admitted that he had to hide his atheism because he felt that people would be terribly shocked and refuse to speak with him if he confessed it. In my case, it seemed very important to tell these women how religion and faith were important to me personally, as a Christian. Although my interlocutors were thoroughly aware that I did not share their relationship to Islam, my religious beliefs made them feel that I could understand their religious experience, or would at least take it seriously.[2] This means that from the point of view of Islam, I am an outsider, but I can also be viewed as an insider because I am a believer. This is especially true for those who were very open to my difference as a Christian, as it was with the disciples of Cemalnur Sargut, who gives great importance to inter-religious dialogue. For some women from other groups, however, the fact that I was a believing Christian had another interesting effect, on which I will elaborate later: I am a more likely convert than a staunch atheist would be.

c. The strength of outsiders: when religion and gender articulate with nationality

When we look at religion and gender as I did previously, we get the impression that, in most cases, even if access is not impossible for outsiders, it is easier for insiders. But there is one characteristic that I would say is easier for outsiders, at least in my field: nationality. Religion, gender and nationality combine in interesting ways.

Religion is a very tricky business in Turkey. Since the founding of the Republic, and even before, secularist trends were in conflict with religious forces. Religious groups, especially Sufi groups, must be very careful in their self-presentation, as they are prone to being criticized – by more conservative groups as being too liberal, or by secularists for being backward and threatening the secular state. Moreover, in Turkey as in other Muslim countries, gender and women's status are central issues for competing views of national identity (Göle 2003; Moghadam 1994). Navigating this complex arena of tensions is easier as a foreigner because one is external to these questions of political identity. It is impossible for a Turkish researcher to claim neutrality in terms of these issues. He or she must have a position on the Turkish politico-religious chessboard, and it can rarely satisfy everyone. Ayşe Saktanber reports the difficulties she has had being accepted in a popular Muslim neighbourhood because of the highly suspicious attitude of its inhabitants toward the secular urban elite. Her initial pilot-study failed because the persons she intended to interview had had many unpleasant

2 It is clear to me that an atheistic anthropologist, if she or he is a good anthropologist, will also take the religious experience of the people she or he studies seriously. However, she or he might have some difficulties convincing them that she or he does so.

experiences with students from her university, which has a reputation for being particularly left wing and opposed to religion (Saktanber 2002).

On the other hand, being religious does not solve the problem for the researcher. This has been experienced by a young Turkish colleague of mine, who is writing her master's thesis on Cemalnur Sargut's disciples. She is a well-trained anthropologist from a good Turkish university; however, she is veiled, whereas Sargut's disciples are not. Although the master shows great respect to women who choose to wear the veil – he told the researcher that her choice to cover or not did not make any difference to the group – the young anthropologist nevertheless felt a strong tension. It is impossible to know if her unease came only from her deep consciousness that she was the only veiled person in the room, or if there was also a reaction from some people in the group. However, this light piece of cloth, symbolizing strong tensions in Turkish society, certainly had an impact on this researcher's interactions with members of the group she studied.[3]

In terms of gender, it seems to me that the issue lies not at the national level, but at a larger one. It is concerned with reciprocal stereotypes of Western and Muslim women. Being a Westerner made me immediately perceived as a feminist, which had some ambiguous effects. Most of the time it was a disadvantage; I felt mistrust, and I had to justify my interest in women by specifying that I had not come with the purpose of proving that Muslim women were oppressed. One woman told me clearly: 'I would not have let you in if I thought you were a feminist.' In my relationship with Cemalnur Sargut, I felt the contrary – that my being a Westerner was sometimes an asset regarding the issue of gender. This female master has progressive views on the role of women in Islam, which she learned from her master, Kenan Rifai, who at the beginning of the twentieth century said that women were the future of religion because they had a greater ability then men to come close to God. These ideas are more widely accepted by Western audiences than in Turkey, as I learned when I once accompanied Sargut on a conference tour in Europe. When I asked her about the talk she would give in Holland a few days later, she told me that she had been invited to speak on the subject of Sufism and women for an audience of Turkish

[3] There are veiled women who come to open classes given by Cemalnur Sargut. They do not seem to feel that there is any problem, but the relationship between researcher and researched is of another kind.

migrants. She sighed and said that she would much prefer a Dutch audience because it was easier for her to speak on this subject to foreigners – and that Turks have trouble understanding her.

These examples demonstrate how difficult it can be to navigate in the Turkish religious context, especially for local researchers, whose situated perspective, be it more or less religious than that of the studied group, is immediately clear and can be perceived as threatening to the respondents. Turkish researchers are quickly categorized because the decisive features that permit their classification are identified right away. This is not the case for foreigners, where a more blurred situation prevails.

A permanent silent negotiation

In the first part of this article, I demonstrated that borders do not always lie where one would expect them, and that various borders can intersect in different ways. I now must complicate this picture a little further. While reflecting on their influence on fieldwork, we should not consider religion or gender as static traits; rather, we should be aware of the continual negotiation that is taking place. That a person's religion is not fixed but can be subject to change is obvious. As I will demonstrate below, the expectation that the researcher's religion can change – or, often, that it should change – creates a large area of negotiation between researcher and respondents during fieldwork. Equally, the ways we conceive gender and the proper behaviours attached to it can vary.

Drawing on the conception of gender developed in a ground-breaking article by West and Zimmerman, I consider that gender is not a feature in itself but something that we perform throughout our daily lives and that is produced in our daily interactions (West and Zimmerman 1987). Gender is not seen as fixed or 'natural' but rather as subject to change and negotiation. Having clarified this, I can complete the sentence of Warren and Hackney that I cited in the introduction by saying that, if gender and religion shape interactions in the field, interactions also shape gender and religion. If we apply this idea to the specific interactions that took place during my research, we see that it is not so much a question of me being fundamentally a woman and a Christian, but of the way in which I presented myself in the interactions and, moreover, of the image that is sent back to me by my respondents.

Indeed, while discussing the question of privileged or hindered access for insiders and outsiders, it would be wrong to think that all is decided once and for all at the first contact. The way the researcher presents herself or himself, how he or she is perceived, what role the researched population allots to her or him – all of these factors evolve during fieldwork and change according to the situation. What characterizes the relationship between the anthropologist and the respondents is that many things remain blurred. First, no matter how hard we try to explain them, our aims will never be completely clear, as the idea of doing research is somehow obscure to many of the people we study. Second, I suspect that both parties find some interest in the situation remaining blurred, because it leaves room for diverse (conscious or unconscious) strategies on both parts. I play with these borders continuously during fieldwork: sometimes stressing my outsider status, sometimes behaving like an insider, and in other instances resisting attempts to make me an insider. Of course, the same could be said of the women I study, who sometimes stress some parts of my identity, constructing me as an outsider, but sometimes stress other characteristics, constructing me as a (partial) insider.

a. Religion

I will begin illustrating this point with the example of the border between Muslims and non-Muslims. Many people whom I have met in various Sufi circles in Istanbul would have liked me to cross the border as soon as possible and become a Muslim myself. It is clear that, for many women, the main reason for accepting me in their midst was the religious merit they would gain if they succeeded in converting me. I have always presented myself as a researcher, but the women I studied often preferred to see me in the role of a potential convert. I must admit that I have the exact profile of a potential convert: a young, Western woman who wants to give religion a more important place in her life but has not yet found the best way to do so. In such a situation, one can ask, after Christel Manning: what happens when the real challenge is not to be accepted by insiders but to maintain your outsidership? (Manning 2001).

As I have mentioned, in some groups this has not been an issue, but in most of those I visited, I have been, to a greater or a lesser extent, the target of pressures to convert to Islam. I often have perceived this situation as very painful, and I have felt distressed by the impression that people would not listen to me when I clearly stated that I had only a scientific interest and no intention of converting. However, I must admit that I sometimes took advantage of this situation, thereby participating in its perpetuation. I have always been clear in what I told them, stressing on each occasion that I was a researcher and nothing more, but my behaviour was more ambiguous, as my interlocutors were prompt to observe. I sometimes acted like the insiders, downplaying all the features that would remind them that I was a researcher trying to gain information. By doing this, I was undermining my own claims to be only a researcher.

For example, I have said previously that I did not take notes at the beginning because I felt that it would create too great a distance. I knew that I would run the risk of them considering me a potential convert by acting like this, but I did it to gain their trust. Sabine Kalinock describes this kind of strategy very well:

> "I rarely used a tape recorder or a camera, for several reasons … … I think I also tried to conform to the women's image of me as a potential convert interested in Islam and not as a researcher (Kalinock 2004, 669)."

It also sometimes happened that, during a friendly discussion with some Sufi women, I would interpret an event from my personal life according to the teachings of their master. While doing this I was aware that I was behaving like an insider, thus blurring my identity as an anthropologist; at the same time, these kind of exchanges were important for my relationship with these women, as I was demonstrating that I understood the teachings that I had been following for months and that I approve of them, at least in part.

b. Gender

The same ambiguity is present in the issue of gender roles and can lead to situations where subtle negotiations occur. On the one hand, in order to be accepted I tried to conform to what I perceived to be adequate behaviour for an insider woman (by veiling during rituals and showing some modesty). On the other hand, I also knew that, as a Westerner, I was expected to have different manners. Moreover, I had to do what was necessary to accomplish my work.

In December 2006, I went on a four-day trip to Konya with a group of Rifai. One evening, we were waiting to have an important *zikr*. As the beginning of the ceremony approached, my friend Fatma and I went to the room where it was going to take place. The room was small, and it was obvious that I had to be quick to secure a seat that would allow me to observe the ritual in an optimal way. It was still early when we arrived, and there were only a few men in the room. I knew that it would not be considered suitable for two young women to sit in the presence of strange men.

Fatma and I hesitated and even asked one of our male dervish friends, who was incidentally passing by, if we could sit down. Because he did not give us a clear answer, we hesitated a bit longer. I became annoyed, until I finally exploded – 'After all, I am European, I don't need to care about these things' – and then sat down. After a while, Fatma stood up, saying that she was going to the lavatory. While I was waiting for her to return, our dervish friend came back and told me to follow him. I though he was going to show me something, but he brought me back upstairs to the main hall, where everyone, including Fatma, was waiting. He was actually showing me that, as a woman, I could not behave in this way, especially when I was deliberately ignoring the rules. He reminded me that, in this instance at least, the rules were valid for all women, Turkish or Western. In this case, I tried to use my outsider status to gain information, but they did not accept it. The interesting point is that when we went down again later, although the room was already packed full with people, Fatma and I somehow ended up seated in exactly the same position I had chosen for us initially. Maybe this had been organized without me noticing, as a reward for having at last followed the rules.

Concluding remarks

In this study, I have elaborated on the diverse implications of the statuses of insider and outsider. I have demonstrated that researchers contribute to a certain confusion concerning their aims and their identities by playing on the different dimensions of their identities at different times in order to be accepted and to collect information – although these misunderstandings can be quite painful. Having said this, I wonder if our interactions with our respondents in the field are difficult because they misunderstand us, or if it would not sometimes be because they understand us too well.

I want to conclude by relating a small incident that illustrates this point. On my first visit to a Qadiri lodge, a woman asked, 'Where are you attached?', by which she meant, 'Which sheikh's disciple are you?'. I answered, 'I am not attached anywhere, *araştırma yapıyorum*, I am doing research', to which she said, '*Ah, arayış içindesin*', which could be translated as, 'I see, you are still searching.' In her reformulation, what I meant as academic research was transformed into a personal quest. I was about to reply to stress the academic dimension of my work – already annoyed that, once again, my aims were being misunderstood – but I refrained. Was she really misunderstanding me? If we take a closer look, pretending just to do research is also a strategy. Its aim is to protect my personal identity, to keep a distance – assuring that I will be able to get close enough to Sufis to study them but remain far enough away to not have my worldview and personal convictions challenged by this experience. I am forced to admit that the woman's understanding was at least as close to the truth as my claim to do research. Yes, I am on a quest. Who can say – especially those working in a religious field – that his or her research is not really a quest? I cannot. Of course, I usually prefer calling it a Ph.D., and having people accept this claim without questioning it.

Bibliography

Abu-Lughod, L. 1988. 'Fieldwork of a dutiful daughter'. In *Arab Women in the Field: Studying Your Own Society* (eds.) S. Altorki and C. Fawzi El-Sohl, 139–61. Syracuse: Syracuse University Press.

Bell, D., P. Caplan and W. J. Karim (eds.). 1993. *Gendered Fields: Women, Men and Ethnography*. London: Routledge.

Caplan, P. 1993. 'Introduction 2: the volume'. In *Gendered Fields: Women, Men and Ethnography* (eds.) D. Bell, P. Caplan and W. J. Karim, 19–27. London; New York: Routledge.

Fathi, H. 2004. *Femmes d'autorité dans l'Asie centrale contemporaine: quête des ancêtres et recompositions identitaires dans l'Islam postsoviétique*. Paris: Maisonneuve et Larose.

Göle, N.2003. *Musulmanes et modernes: voile et civilisation en Turquie*. Paris: La Découverte.

Gregory, J. R. 1984. 'The myth of the male ethnographer and the woman's world'. *American Anthropologist* 86, no. 2: 316–27.

Haraway, D. J. 1988. 'Situated knowledges: the science question in feminism and the privilege of partial perspective'. *Feminist Studies* 14, no. 3: 575–99.

Hegland, M. E. 2003. 'Shia women's rituals in northwest Pakistan: the shortcomings and significance of resistance'. *Anthropological Quarterly* 76, no. 3: 411–42.

Kalinock, S.2004. 'Touching a sensitive topic: research in Shiite rituals of women in Tehran'. *Iranian Studies* 37, no. 4: 665–74.

Manning, C. 2001. 'Conversations among women: gender as a bridge between religious and ideological cultures'. In *Toward Reflexive Ethnography: Participating, Observing, Narrating* (eds.) D. G. Bromley and L. F. Carter, 117–32. Amsterdam: Jai.

Moghadam, V. M. 1994. *Gender and National Identity: Women and Politics in Muslim Societies*. London: Zed Books.

Raudvere, C. 2002. *The Book and the Roses: Sufi Women, Visibility, and Zikir in Contemporary Istanbul*. Istanbul: Swedish Research Institute Istanbul.

Saktanber, A. 2002. *Living Islam: Women, Religion and the Politicization of Culture in Turkey*. London: I. B. Tauris.

Warren, C. A. B., and J. K. Hackney. 2000. *Gender Issues in Ethnography*. Thousand Oaks, CA: Sage.

Werbner, P. 2003. *Pilgrims of Love: The Anthropology of a Global Sufi Cult*. London: Hurst and Company.

West, C., and D. Zimmerman. 1987. 'Doing gender'. *Gender and Society* 1, no. 2: 125–51.

Women transferring Shia rituals in western Migrancy

Ingvild Flaskerud

Introduction

Studies of Muslim migration to the West suggest that Muslims do not practice their religion in Europe and the U.S. exactly as they do in their native lands – and that Western-born Muslims individu'ali ze and modernize their religious practices (Cesari 2004, 80–92). In this essay, I discuss the ways in which the ritual fabric of women's *'Ashura* commemoration – and the meaning of ritual participation – is shaped by new sociocultural circumstances in a small Shiite migrant environment in Norway.[1] *'Ashura,* which commemorates the battle at Karbala, is one of the most important religious festivals in the Shia liturgical year. The festival begins on the first of Muharram and culminates on the tenth, *'Ashura* .

One consequence of migration is the transfer of rituals from localities characterized by a long Shia history to a small migrant community with no Shia history. In the new context, the size of the community, along with its noninstitutional, multicultural and multinational character, influences social agents' choices in designing *'Ashura* commemorations. As a result, the reestablishment of the ritual practice corresponds to observations made by Langer and his colleagues, who, in their discussion of the transfer of rituals, suggest that the process may involve modification, invention and disappearance (Langer, Lüddeckens, Radde, and Snoek 2006). Bell has, however, identified certain challenges that processes of change pose to a

[1] Ethnographic information is based on interviews and participant observation in a small Shiite community in northern Norway (Tromso), located above the Arctic Circle. The research period spanned from 2005 to 2008.

religious community. It may, for example, face the question of the degree to which people can tamper with ritual traditions before the authority and dignity of these traditions are undermined (Bell 1997, 172). Studies of Muslim migration to the West suggest several responses to globalization and multiculturalism. Syncretism – the infiltration of a supposedly 'pure' tradition by symbols and meanings seen as belonging to other, incompatible traditions – might be seen as threatening the religious identity of the individual and the community (Stewart and Shaw 1994). Some Muslims respond to syncretism with 'ethnification', reconstituting themselves along ethnic lines and defending an ethnic vision of Islam rooted in their respective national cultures of origin. On the other hand, globalization and the development of transnational networks have motivated a different process, oriented toward the 'purification' of Islamic tradition by detaching Islam from any given culture, a process called 'deculturation' (Roy 2004). A third response is to revise and recreate Islamic culture by hybridising Muslim heritage with the dominant norms and values in the host society (Cesari 2004).

Muharram commemoration ceremonies typically present culturally developed methods and practices for expressing collective religious beliefs and individual devotion. A central issue related to the reestablishment of rituals in a multicultural and multinational migrant context is the extent to which a ritual might continue to be perceived as meaningful to its participants when methods and practices change. My analysis draws on memory and ritual studies, particularly the relationship between ritual tradition and collective and individual memory, to discuss the reformulation of religious tradition horizontally, across cultural borders, and vertically, across generations.

Societal characteristics

The community discussed here consists of people originating from Iraq, Iran, Afghanistan and India who belong to the Twelver branch of Shiism. Some arrived in Norway in the early 1990s; others arrived more recently. The various individuals in this study are, to different degrees, integrated into the social fabric of the society. Among the adults, some are professionals, others are students and still others are connected to public programmes for the rehabilitation of refugees. Children and teenagers are enrolled in state-run kindergartens and schools. The adults' proficiency in Norwegian varies from fluent to less competent. The younger generation generally performs better and typically uses Norwegian to communicate among themselves. Adults from Iraq, Iran and Afghanistan typically use Persian to communicate with each other but must use Norwegian or English to include those from India.

The Shias have settled in various parts of Tromso. They do not form an organized community, and there is no formal leadership. Rather, it is a self-selected group, consisting of about ten families who have organized themselves on the basis of informal networking through friendship.[2] Whereas the Shias tend to be marginalized or excluded by the Sunnis, they are disregarded by the general Norwegian population, who do not know much about them due to their low public visibility as Shias.

Practical attempts to re-establish Muharram commemoration

The community has faced certain practical challenges in its attempt to re-establish Muharram commemoration. The Norwegian social framework combines a State Lutheran Church with a secular, social democratic ideology. The state provides financial support to the Lutheran church but guarantees freedom of religion by also supporting other religious and philosophical societies. Subsidies are granted to those societies according to membership numbers, which are reported to the authorities annually. Mosques receive financial support according to this system. In addition, members are asked to pay membership fees. Sometimes a mosque also receives grants from private donors or religious associations in the Muslim heartlands.[3] The Shia community under consideration, however, is not registered as a religious community and does not receive any financial support from the State; it also does not receive funding from private donors. The group's financial needs are not pressing, but some financial support could help address the ongoing challenge of finding a location for rituals and festivals. The group is not in need of a location at their permanent disposal but would appreciate a space available to rent for certain occasions. This venue should be spacious enough to host rituals for men and women that are held simul-

[2] By contrast, in 2009 there were nine Shia Muslim cultural associations in Oslo, many organized according to national or linguistic borders.

[3] See, for example, Amal-Naguib 2002.

taneously, in separate rooms. Moreover, there should be facilities such as a kitchen and bathrooms.[4]

In 2005 the community organized mourning commemoration in a private home that was large enough to host men and women in separate rooms. In 2006 the owners changed their location and could no longer host rituals. Some of the Shias were members of one of the two local mosques. Male representatives negotiated with the two mosques in town concerning the possibility of arranging rituals in these locations. Leaders of the al-Nur mosque, supported with money from Saudi Arabia, responded negatively in this regard. Leaders of the independent al-Rahman mosque were ambiguous but rejected the Shia community shortly before the ritual festival. When the mosques were unable or unwilling to provide the necessary service to the Shia community, most Shias withdrew their memberships. The Shia community then approached the municip'Ali ty to ask for help in finding a suitable location, but with no results. As a consequence, no communal ritual was organized in 2006. In 2007 male representatives of the Shia community approached various private and public institutions, seeking to rent a location. Eventually, they were able to rent the meeting place of a public youth association, having at their disposal separate rooms for men's and women's rituals, a kitchen and bathrooms. The men met in the communal hall and the women gathered in the spacious kitchen, from which they could also supervise the preparation of a meal to be served at the end of the ceremony.

When the community negotiated with Muslim institutions and Norwegian authorities, men acted as representatives of the community. However, women played a role behind the scenes. Men and women would organize gender-specific rituals, but collaboration between the two sexes was necessary to ensure family-oriented rituals. Before the men met with the authorities, the issues they were to raise had been discussed in the community's homes in order to clarify the needs of the whole group. At a later stage, women were in charge of designing the programme for their ceremony, which also included minor children and female teenagers. Decisions were typically made via telephone because many women were working or studying during the day and engaged in various activities in the evenings:

---

4 In larger towns more numerous Shia communities host rituals in *husayniyyeh*. See Strandhagen 2008.

those related to personal well-being, such as physical training, or related to child-raising, such as schoolwork and accompanying children to leisure activities.

'Ashura in Shia piety

The *'Ashura* ritual tradition combines text-based and popular religion. Historically and geographically, the structure and meaning of rituals have been subject to change and invention. Rituals have, however, evolved around the core dogmas related to the position of Imam'Ali as the righteous leader of the Muslim *ummah* after the death of the Prophet Muhammad in 632 A.D., and the role of the following eleven Imams as authorized interpreters of the Quran (due to their particular knowledge of its esoteric and exoteric meanings). The belief in Imam Hoseyn as the wronged martyr fighting for the true understanding of Islam at the battle of Karbala in 680 A.D. is also central. Shia theology has built on this event to develop a martyrology that connects the suffering of Imam Hoseyn and his supporters with a soteriology focused on redemptive suffering (Ayoub 1978.). The wronged martyrs are believed to have been rewarded by God with the ability to act as intercessors between the divine and the pious. The pious, on their part, can appeal to intercessors and promote redemption by commemorating Hoseyn's sacrifice, expressing condolence and continuing to support the way of God as transmitted by the Prophet and the Imams.

This dogma is enacted through ritual performances in which the pious mourn the suffering of the martyrs. Mourning is embodied in various ways, such as reading and listening to lamentation poetry, weeping and flagellation. These rites are considered to be meritorious, offering *savab*. In contemporary Shia communities, ritual performance continues to be the result of believers' conscious creation, modification and choice on the basis of ideas about how to make a ritual work and in response to political changes (Deeb 2005; Deeb 2006).

Cultural complexity and transnational experiences

In the past, Shias in the migrant community have had varied opportunities to express their religious sentiments in a communal public setting. The

Shias originating from India and Afghanistan have been accustomed to negotiating their presence in a Hindu or Sunni majority environment but have nevertheless benefited culturally from belonging to a Shia community that could offer religious services to its members. The Shias originating from Iraq come from a Shia majority society, in which Shia belief and traditions have thrived but have been constrained under Sunni/secular rule. The migrants originating from Iran have benefited from living in a state that endorses Shia ritual and belief, although their religious lives were, to some extent, controlled by the State's particular Islamist ideology.

Despite being separated by national borders, members of Shia communities have frequently engaged in formal and informal transnational networks. It is, however, apparent that the members of the community in this study are not necessarily familiar with each other's culturally specific forms of commemoration. This diversity may pose a challenge when attempting to establish a common ground for ritual performance. In this process, many Iraqis and Afghans drew upon previous migrant experience in Iran, where they lived before settling in Norway. The Iraqi spent several years as refugees in Iran as a consequence of the war between Iran and Iraq (1980–88), whereas the Afghans fled the civil war in Afghanistan, which raged between 1989, when the Soviet occupation ended, and 1995, when the Taliban movement consolidated its control over the country. In Iran they had been integrated into civil society while simultaneously forming distinct social and ritual networks as well as organizing commemoration ceremonies using their native language and performing local costumes. Nevertheless, many developed a familiarity with the modes of ritual performance of the Iranian post-revolutionary era, which established a common frame of reference in the Norwegian migrant setting. Only the Indian group was unfamiliar with Iranian-style Muharram commemoration. Their north Indian ritual heritage draws on Shia traditions introduced in the eighteenth century but has taken its own course of development.

As for contemporary Iranian Muharram traditions, it should be noted that although these traditions are taken as the group's common ground, performative designs may vary across Iran. The styles with which the social agents in this study have become familiar are practiced in Tehran and northern Iran. Studies on commemoration-related rituals in Iran since the late 1970s have noted two tendencies. On the one hand, rituals present an arena for spiritual consolation; on the other hand, they are an arena for political and social protest and involvement (Hegland 1983, 218–35; Thaiss 1972, 349–66). Although one approach does not necessarily exclude the other, the two may be classified as quietist and activist, respectively. Studies concentrating on the post-revolutionary era demonstrate the continuation of politicized, as well as spiritually oriented, rituals (Kalinock 2003a; Kalinock 2003b; Torab 2007; Torab 2002). Young adult Shia migrants to Norway, having grown up or lived as refugees in Iran, have been exposed to these tendencies. It is, however, evident that the ritual formation in the migrant community in this study was not oriented toward political issues but concentrated on spiritual and redemptive aspects of Muharram commemoration. Nationalism is not accentuated, and cultural differences are respected.

Ritual performance

In order to develop a working ritual setting in this particular social circumstance, the Shias need to negotiate a common frame of reference and attend to issues such as liturgy and language. Liturgy may be understood as a defined ritual performance organized according to some structuring principle. These structuring principles refer to the totality of cult behaviour and involve speech, recitation and song as well as movements and the use of specific symbols and colours (Sinding-Larsen 1984, 20). Liturgy differs from private devotion, which is performed outside the realm of these structuring principles – for example, immediately before or after the liturgy, or completely disconnected from liturgy, outside the ritual proper. Another distinction between liturgy and private devotion is that liturgy is performed collectively, whereas private devotion is an individual act; believers' participation in liturgy might, however, contain moments of personal devotional intentions and actions.

The quietist approach to Muharram ritual performance in Iran typically follows a certain structure. A ceremony would start with the ritual leader inviting the congregation to join him in praising and greeting God, the Prophet Muhammad and his descendants (*salavat*) and with recitation from the Quran, followed by a lecture (*khutbeh*) by a *mullah*. Next, there would be a collective reading from the Shia prayer manual 'Keys to the Garden of Heaven' (*Mafatih al-Jenan*). A ritual leader (*maddah*) would narrate stories about the wronged martyrs at the battle at Karbala, called *rowzeh*, and perform elegies (*nowheh*) while the congregation participated with flagellation and lamentation, to be followed by the presentation of supplications (*du'a*). The ritual would end with thanksgivings (*nazri*), typically in the form of a meal shared by everyone present. At this point, the spiritual and social aspects typical of Shia rituals merge. These are also essential elements of commemoration rituals in Iraq, Afghanistan and India, although in each country, and even in different regions of a country, local liturgical and aesthetic expressions have developed.

The primary challenge facing the migrant community in this study was the lack of ritual expertise. In 2007 this situation resulted in certain modifications to both men's and women's rituals. The community did not have access to a *mullah,* and the lecture was omitted.[5] A lecture is not, however, the most distinct rite connected to lamentation in Muharram. More important are the collective recitation of the prayer *ziyarat 'Ashura* and the performance of *rowzeh* and *nowheh* under the leadership of a *maddah*. One of the central roles of a *maddah*, when performing *rowzeh* and *nowheh*, is to bring ritual participants into a state of mourning so that they can express sympathy with and allegiance to the martyred at Karbala and be placed in the position of receiving God's grace (*fiyz-i illahi*). In principle, ritual participants can receive God's grace by listening to the tragic story of Karbala and becoming emotionally involved. Typically, a ritual leader would try to achieve this by manipulating her or his voice to enhance the sense of drama. The women in this study lacked competence in the *maddah*'s skills. Many had left their countries of origin when they were still young, before having the opportunity to develop skills in telling *rowzeh* and leading *nowheh*. By comparison, my fieldwork concerning Muharram ceremonies in Iran between 1999 and 2003 demonstrated that not all ritual participants are equally competent in performance skills.[6] It is not surprising that patterns of compartmentalized knowledge should be repeated in a migrant context.

The women's ritual performance concentrated instead on reading the

---

5 Larger Shia communities in the capital, Oslo, can invite mullahs to speak in *husayniyyeh* during Muharram commemoration rituals. In some places, the *mullah* will speak to mixed-gender audiences. In gender-segregated gatherings he will present his lecture in the men's section, which is monitored [watched?] by women on a projector screen.

6 This is why the ritual leader (*maddah*) who performs the *rowzeh* is usually supported by a group of assistants (*zakir*) who guide the congregation through the ceremony: responsorial songs, the various forms of ritual dance, and flagellation.

pilgrims' prayer *ziyarat 'Ashura* and the supplication *du'ay-i tawassul*, which are part of Iranian, Iraqi, Afghan and Indian Muharram commemorations. Small booklets containing a selection of commonly used prayers from *Mafatih al-Jenan* were distributed among the women, seated on carpets on the kitchen floor, who took turns reading. *Ziyarat 'Ashura* is part of the liturgy developed for the pilgrimage to Imam Hoseyn's shrine at Karbala. Not every Shia will have the opportunity to visit Karbala, and a pilgrimage can be performed symbolically.[7] Whoever recites *ziyarat 'Ashura* is said to enjoy the status of the martyrs at Karbala and to be rewarded alongside those who go to Karbala to perform the pilgrimage. *Ziyarat 'Ashura* is also used as a supplication *(du'a)* and is considered to be particularly beneficial. *Du'ay-i tavassul* is among the most popular Shia supplications. It calls upon the saints to intercede, speaking before God in the believer's favour to obtain pardon and deliverance from sins. Moreover, taking turns reading the prayers allows ritual participants to promote their personal merit (*savab*). Some of the senior women cried silently while the prayers were read. Among the younger women, some could follow the text in Arabic, whereas to others the words were incomprehensible; they had little knowledge of the prayers' content and purpose. Only one elegy, *nowheh*, was performed. It was sung in Urdu by an Indian woman. The literal meaning was incomprehensible to most listeners; however, the repeated mentions of Zaynab (Imam Hoseyn's sister, who was important in preserving the memory of the battle at Karbala and protecting its ideals) and the sad melody accompanying the lyrics generated lamentation and weeping among several senior ritual participants. By invoking the name of Zaynab in that context, the memory of Karbala was evoked in the adult audience, drawing on familiarity with the content of the Karbala narrative and knowledge of ritual reward. Then the researcher was invited to give a short lecture on the meaning of the battle of Karbala. After a lively discussion among the adult women, the ceremony concluded with a votive meal consisting of dishes from the four countries of origin. While eating and chatting, the women and children could watch, on a television screen, a home video made by

7 The fifth Imam, Muhammad bin Ali al-Baqir, is reported to have taught a certain al-Qamah ibn Muhammad to perform a symbolic visit to Karbala. Among his recommendations was reciting *ziyarat 'Ashura* while facing Karbala on the day of *'Ashura*.(*Call on Me, I Answer You*, 207). Another rewarding action was holding a mourning session (*matam*) and inviting family and friends to attend. See Ayoub 1978, 188–89.

Indian members of the community. During the ceremony, the smaller children had been running between the male and female spaces, spending short periods of time in each and playing in the corridor.

In the migrant context, the liturgy was modified and reduced to meet the ability of the adult participants.[8] Many young adult women did, however, find it difficult to participate in this modified and limited liturgy. In particular, those who had lived many years in Norway lacked liturgical competence, and some found it difficult to become engaged from the perspective of personal devotion. The Karbala event and its importance to Islam, as well as to their own personal salvation, were perceived as somewhat alien. Many young women perceived the votive meal following the commemoration to be a social event rather than a religious thanksgiving.

The ritual as a site for religious instruction

The need for religious instruction for women, young female adults and children was recognised by some women, who took steps to improve the situation. The Muharram ritual became a site of education for the multicultural community in two respects: learning about each other's traditions and shaping a common ground for ritual performance, and teaching the younger generation about Shiism. In their countries of origin, belief and dogma are transmitted through various channels, such as formal religious education in seminars, school curricula and the performance of rituals. Framed in the orthodox code of belief, ritual performance is shaped by local tradition, social circumstances, and individual initiative and creativity – and transmitted to, and acquired by, new generations through observation and participation. A particular challenge faced by the migrant community in this study was the question of how to inform the younger generation about Shia belief and ritual practice – and invite them to contemplate its significance and relevance in relation to their own lives.

8 Another example of modifications made due to a lack of trained performers can be found among South Asian Muslims in Canada. They have turned to *qawwali* recordings to evoke the experience of *sama'*, or retreated to *zikr*. Qureishi describes the general tendency as a transition from performance, which includes traditional service professions and which projects domination, submission and temporal-spatial coordination within the group, to participation, in which everyone's voice is included, but no one dominates. Qureshi 1996, 61.

The women chose to employ new didactic strategies by inviting the researcher to share her knowledge about Shiism with the women, young adult females and children. On the day of the commemoration in 2005, I was asked to show an ethnographic film I had made about women commemorating *'Ashura* in Shiraz (Flaskerud 2003). The film was shown on the television screen in the living room of the hosting family. The film gives a brief introduction to the battle of Karbala as a sacred event in Shiite history. It then describes women commemorating the event through various types of ritual performances and presents interviews with a ritual leader and two hostesses. The film provoked a discussion about tradition among the women. Some of the information in the film was new to Iranians from northern Iran, as well as to people from Iraq, Afghanistan and India. They did, nevertheless, recognise various rites from their home settings, such as the type of flagellation known as *sinehzani*, although the choreography would differ geographically. A discussion arose over ritual form, but ritual intention was given prominence. One woman pointed out that ritual action should 'come from the heart'; if ritual action was instigated from the heart, it would be intense in expression and therefore forceful. It was acknowledged in the group that such expressive performance and participation was dependent on skills. One would need a good leader and a group of ritual participants who knew the choreography and would be focused in intention and commitment.

For the commemoration in 2007, I was asked to give a lecture to the young female adults and children in Norwegian. It was thought that my knowledge of Islamic history, my command of Norwegian and my familiarity with the critical-reflexive pedagogic typical of a Western education would enable me to speak about the significance of the battle at Karbala in a manner that would be discernible considering the mind-set of their Western-influenced children. Using PowerPoint software, I presented images of colourful posters purchased in Iran, showing imaginary portraits of Imam 'Ali and visual narrations of the battle at Karbala and its aftermath. I connected Imam Hoseyn's mission at Karbala to the vocation of his father Imam 'Ali and framed their efforts in the theology of the Imamate and the belief in redemptive suffering. I continued by giving examples of the ways in which the battle at Karbala is commemorated today by presenting photographs I had taken in Iran, showing men, women and children participating in various ritual practices. The lecture lasted about fifteen minutes.

As in 2005, my introduction of ritual practices in Iran sparked a discussion among the women about traditions in various countries and the meaning of ritual performance. They recognized the different cultural expressions of Shiism and did not seem hostile to variations, as they could agree on core dogmas. The young adults remained silent during the discussion.

The modification of liturgy and the meaning of ritual participation

The individual Shias who engaged in creating a communal *'Ashura* commemoration shared a belief in the importance of keeping the memory of Karbala alive – and thus keeping alive a certain way of living as Muslims. The ceremony was perceived to be merciful and generous, and to offer God's grace through Imam Hoseyn's example. It would help the believers to find the right way – that is, how to live as human beings and help those in need. One of the greatest challenges in pursuing this goal was the lack of both competence and a shared common ground for ritual participation. In the process of re-creating a commemoration ritual in a multicultural and multinational sociocultural context, the ritual fabric was reduced to reading prayers, listening to a short performance of *nowheh*, and sharing an ex-votive meal. These rites are, however, central to one of the important purposes of *'Ashura* commemoration: communicating with the divine (through the intercession of saints) via prayer, invocations and thanksgivings.

The introduction of a lecture by an outsider, framed in the historical-critical approach of Western academia, was an innovative move. The lecture replaced the hagiographic narration of *rowzeh* and provided a different approach to religious understanding than the normative and devout approach of a theologian. How did the ritual participants perceive these modifications and innovations?

When reviewing the ritual later, the women acknowledged that they had changed its fabric but argued that it is not important to perform the ritual exactly as it is performed in their countries of origin. Most importantly, they felt, they should do what is within their ability to create a spiritual environment (*ruhani kardan*), evoking within each individual a sincere (*khalesaneh*) and devotional (*ekhlas*) feeling that would allow them to speak and connect with the Imams. They admitted that the current year (2007) had been difficult. The liturgy had been short and the children had diverted their attention. In order to improve the situation the following year, it was suggested that they share knowledge and resources with the men. They reasoned that by placing a microphone in the men's section, they could listen to the men's *rowzeh*. They also could write a *rowzeh* (in Persian) known to one of the senior women and invite a young male teenager to recite it, as it would not be decent for a woman recite in front of the men. The representative significance of Shia lamentation rites and liturgical objects – and their roles as modes of engaging with the divine and creating sacred space – are well documented (Chelkowski 1986; Chelkowski 1989; Chelkowski 1996; Flaskerud 2005; Flaskerud 2004; Hyder 2006). The above reasoning supports such functions of liturgy but also underlines the importance of the believer's intention when engaging in ritual participation. When the intention is sincere, participation will be rewarded.

The understanding of what generates a favourable spiritual feeling not only was connected to liturgical aspects but also included factors specific to the sociocultural migrant situation, such as the importance of creating a community and addressing the absence of family and longtime friends. Organizing a ritual, even a commemoration ritual, was perceived as something positive that brought people together, made them happy and created the sense of belonging to a community. It was pointed out that religious merit (*savab*) is attained not simply through lamenting and mourning but also through doing something positive for the religion and for other people. In the process, the participants would set aside cultural and national differences and think of themselves as Muslims. One woman explained, 'How you proceed in the rite is a private matter. We have a common goal and the specific variety of method will not stand in its way.' Therefore, it was accepted that everyone contributed in her own way – for example, by preparing food characteristic of her country of origin – and that such participation would position each woman to accrue religious merit (*savab*).

In addition to strengthening the sense of belonging to a community in migrancy, the act of organizing rituals encouraged mental bonding to communities left behind. *'Ashura* commemoration not only stimulated the memory of martyrs at a historical battle but also evoked personal memories of friends and families. Organizing rituals thus generated feelings of spiritual comfort and inner peace. This feeling also could be created in the country of origin, but the sensation was enhanced in migrancy because of the absence of family and friends.

Collective and individual memory and the transfer of ritual

When attempting to maintain a Shia identity, a small multinational and multicultural minority is faced with the challenge of negotiating a common platform for shared religious belief while also allowing for individual understanding. The social actors in this study acknowledged the relationship between religion and culture and attempted to reformulate the ritual of commemoration around traditional expressions from several Shia cultures. These expressions were perceived as means of articulating belief and communicating with the divine. By stressing the importance of intention, the social agents were able to accept various forms of Shia cultural expression. In conversations about transmitting Shia identity to second-generation migrants, it was perceived as positive that the children learned about different cultural expressions of Shiism around the world. Through observation, it was held, they would learn how to pray and to offer thanksgivings (*nazri*) and be informed about sacred history. The children then were expected to be able to choose methods of ritual practice that would suit them as individuals. These findings are contrary to understandings of the 'ethnification' of Islam in Western migrancy and 'deculturation' (Roy 2004, 120). In the present study, religion and religiosity are expressed through cultural formulas, not isolated from them. Instead of promoting one national or ethnic cultural tradition as authentic, the group recognizes Shiism as a multicultural phenomena.

One important premise for the continued support and promotion of religious traditions is the way in which they relate to collective and individual memory. The task of collective memory, according to Assmann, is to transmit collective identity (Assmann 2006, 6–7). Collective and individual memory turn to the archive of cultural traditions and the arsenal of symbolic forms, myths and images. Cultural memory is thus a basis for both collective and individual memory. According to Hervieu-Léger, religion implies that collective memory is mobilized (Hervieu-Léger 2006, 124). Religious tradition is like a chain of belief, and whether a group or an individual sees itself as part of a chain or lineage depends on the mentions of the past and the memories that are consciously shared with and passed along to others (Hervieu-Léger 2006, 123). The collective identity of the ritual community in migration thus is dependent on the community being able to perpetuate that chain of belief. Sociological studies of modernization and secularization have suggested that such processes of change make societies less and less able to project a lineage of belief, to the extent that they are no longer societies of memory. Hervieu-Léger argues, however, that the normative and collective religious memory is reinforced by the fact of the group defining itself, objectively and subjectively, as a lineage of belief (Hervieu-Léger 2006, 125). Its formation and reproductiveness spring entirely from cultural memory, which is more extensive than the memory of any particular group, feeding this self-definition. Several scholars suggest that memories of the past are conveyed and sustained by ritual performance. Assmann and Hervieu-Léger locate the recalling of the past, the practice of anamnesis, to the rite, and Connerton argues that calendrical rites and their commemoration serve as 'acts of transfer' of social memory within a social group (Assmann 2006, 9–11; Hervieu-Léger 2006, 125; Connerton 1989, 43).

The historical battle at Karbala, phrased in the mythical language of hagiographic narration and commemorated in diverse cultural expressions throughout history, is central to Shia collective memory. Hagiography and ritual practices are fundamental to the religious memory of the redemptive power of the event, whereas the memory of redemption encourages the survival of ritual practices such as *'Ashura*. The collective religious memory is thus a source from which the women can draw when reconstructing the *'Ashura* ritual in migrancy. The collective memory does, however, exist more like an abstract idea than a social reality. In the multicultural migrant environment, ritual practices drawing from the collective memory take on culturally specific forms of *'Ashura* ritual performance that are not socially shared. The composition of the ritual is, therefore, modified when compared to familiar patterns of ritual performance in countries of origin. This transformation, including the disappearance of some rites, nevertheless allows the women to engage in the ritual and benefit from its grace. The women's practices thus represent a continuation of the chain of belief. I argue that one important premise for such continuation is the way the women are able to connect individual memories to the collective memory. While engaging in the ritual, first-generation migrants can mentally expand the present ritual space to include memories of rituals performed in their countries of origin and in countries in which they lived as refugees before arriving in Norway. Ritual experience in the present was connected to ritual experience in the past, such as the memory of performative patterns and liturgy and the understanding of certain rites and words. Mentioning the name Zaynab had the power to recall the faith of Hoseyn's sister to the minds of the ritual performers – and to represent her. Emotional expressions of lamentation were motivated by previous experiences of belonging to passionate ritual communities. By connecting individual memories to collective memories, a feeling of continuity and belonging was established.

It is however, important to distinguish between the roles of individual memory for first- and second-generation migrants. Many young adult women of the second generation lacked knowledge of the Shia collective memory. Those who had such knowledge found it difficult to connect their individual memories to the redemptive powers of Karbala, due to their short life experiences.[9] They did not participate actively in the ritual, nor did they seem to be particularly moved by it. Instead, the second-generation migrants must create memories through new contexts of religious socialization and life experience. The findings in the present study do not divert from Asad's reflections on tradition, which by now have become axiomatic. He suggests that tradition is not necessarily imitation of earlier practices, because 'it will be the practitioners' conceptions of what is apt performance, and of how the past is related to present practices, that will be crucial for tradition, not the apparent repetition of an old form' (Asad 1986, 15). What I have done is analyze how such processes occur, with specific attention to women transferring rituals in multicultural migrant contexts.

Concluding remarks

Historically, the structure and the meaning of *'Ashura* commemoration rituals have been fluid. Observations of the ways in which Shia rituals offer a symbolic language for interpreting the past and the present, and how rituals are shaped by sociological and political settings, are made, for example, by Hegland (1997) and Torab (2002, 2007) in Iran; Deeb (2005) in Lebanon;

---

[9] Similar processes among young Iraqi women immigrants to Denmark are discussed in Pedersen 2009, 129–30. This should not, however, be perceived as a phenomenon particular to migrancy, as many young women expressed the same ideas to me when I conducted field research in Iran between 1999 and 2003.

Abbas (2002) and Pinault (2001) in Pakistan; Blomfield (2008) in the USA; Spellmann (2004) in England; and Pedersen (2009) in Denmark.

Since the 1960s quietist and activist interpretations of Imam Hoseyn's martyrdom at Karbala have lived side by side in Iran, resulting in different ritual structures (Thaiss 1972; Hegland 1983). A quietist interpretation would result in a ritual structure giving privilege to lamentation rites, whereas an activist interpretation gives privilege to the lecture, which was loaded with religious ideology and endorsed political engagement. A similar response to changing social and political circumstances can be found in Lebanon: an 'authenticated' interpretation of *'Ashura* has challenged a traditional interpretation. This has been especially true since the 1970s, as a response to civil war, occupation by Israel, political marginalization of the Shia and economic decline. The result has been a change to the ritual structure, in which the lecture now is privileged above lamentation rites (Deeb 2005). Discussing Indian Shia mourning practices in a migrant community in the USA, Akbar Hyder similarly identifies various discourses regarding Muharram practices and rituals. He suggests that ritual practice is shaped by, for example, aesthetic conditions, established conventions, epistemological orientation, patronage patterns and larger ideological forces that shape the narrative of Karbala in India and the USA. Exploring the ways in which a ritual serves to historicize Karbala, Hyder highlights the ways in which ritual participants bring to the fore a variety of social concerns.

Normative debates on 'correct' ritual practices are not uncommon, but ritual practices and their interpretation may undergo modification as long as they appear meaningful in a given socio-political context. In fact, rituals sometimes must change in order to preserve their authority as meaningful in new social circumstances. In the quest to establish a new ritual community, the women in the present study acted reflectively and strategically. The story about the battle at Karbala was perceived as constituting the collective memory of the group. In the process of ascertaining this memory, the women drew on Shia cultural sources as well as outside competence. They agreed on a common ground regarding the meaning of core belief and the intended spiritual merit gained from participating in mourning rituals. They acknowledged differences in cultural expressions and believed they would benefit spiritually from participating in unfamiliar rites. These elements will be part of the new collective memory created in the group and will shape individual memories. When discussing religious identity and the

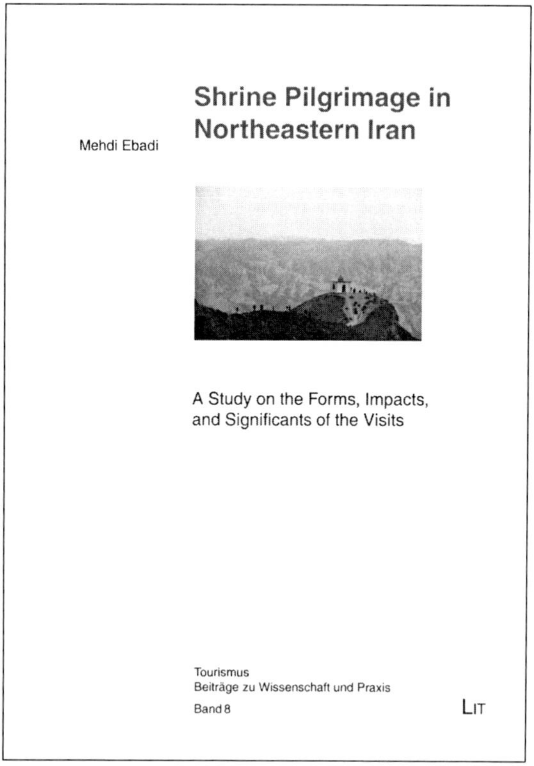
Mehdi Ebadi
Shrine Pilgrimage in Northeastern Iran
A Study on the Forms, Impacts, and Significants of the Visits
Tourismus
Beiträge zu Wissenschaft und Praxis
Band 8
LIT

Asghar Tahmasebi
Pastoral Vulnerability to Socio-political and Climate Stresses
The Shahsevan of North Iran

This book analyses the social and economic situation of mountain nomads in the harsh ecological environment of northwestern Iran. Based on in-depth field work and living with the nomads for a whole year, the author succeeds to give a vivid insight into the Shahsevans' strategy to cope with both political impacts and changing environmental conditions of their traditional way of life. At the same time, this study reveals the intensity of climatic change and the nomads' adaptation measures to these ecological threats. It is a well documented and comprehensive analysis of the interactions between nature and societies under stress. As such, this book and its content can serve as a model for urgently needed comparative studies in the mountain belts of Western and Central Asia.

ZEF Development Studies, Bd. 22, 2013, 192 S., 29,90 €, br., ISBN 978-3-643-90357-0

LIT Verlag Berlin – Münster – Wien – Zürich – London

Auslieferung Deutschland / Österreich / Schweiz: siehe Impressumsseite